Perugia, Italy Travel Guide 2023: Cuisine, Craft Your Perfect Itinerary for an Unforgettable Perugia Adventure

Lorenzo Itinerante

PERUGIA
ITALY
TRAVEL GUIDE

2023

Hidden Gems, Art and Culture, Savoring Local Cuisine, Craft Your
Perfect Itinerary for an Unforgettable Perugia Adventure

LORENZO ITINERANTE

Table of Contents

Three Days in Perugia and Beyond: Unveiling the Treasures of Perugia and Umbria

Chapter 1: Introduction to Perugia

Welcome to Perugia: A City of Timeless Charm

Nestled amidst the rolling hills of central Italy's Umbria region, Perugia beckons travelers with its irresistible allure. Welcome to a city steeped in history, art, and culture, where ancient traditions merge seamlessly with modern life. As you step into the heart of Perugia, you'll find yourself enchanted by the cobblestone streets, charming piazzas, and a sense of timelessness that permeates every corner.

Perugia, the capital of Umbria, boasts a rich heritage dating back to the Etruscan era. As you wander through its streets, you'll encounter traces of the past that have gracefully stood the test of time. The city's Etruscan origins are evident in the majestic archways, the remnants of ancient walls, and the secret underground passages that whisper stories of bygone days.

A highlight of your journey will undoubtedly be the captivating Piazza IV Novembre, the beating heart of Perugia. This bustling square lies at the center of the city, and its focal point is the magnificent Fontana Maggiore, an exquisite medieval fountain adorned with intricate sculptures and reliefs. Here, locals and visitors gather, savoring the vibrant atmosphere while soaking in the grandeur of the historical landmarks that surround the square.

Art enthusiasts will find themselves in paradise at the Galleria Nazionale dell'Umbria, a treasure trove of masterpieces from renowned Italian artists like Perugino, Pinturicchio, and Raphael.

The gallery's rich collection is a testament to the city's significant role in Italy's artistic legacy, and it offers an opportunity to immerse oneself in the captivating world of Italian Renaissance art.

As the sun sets over the rolling hills, Perugia's charm takes on a different hue. The city comes alive with a dynamic energy as locals and visitors spill into the charming alleys and vibrant nightlife spots. You'll discover cozy wine bars where you can savor the region's finest wines, intimate cafes perfect for sipping espresso while people-watching, and traditional trattorias serving mouthwatering Umbrian delicacies.

Perugia's allure isn't limited to its historic center alone. The city's modern spirit is evident in its dynamic cultural scene and thriving student population. The prestigious University for Foreigners draws students from around the world, lending a cosmopolitan vibe to the city.

Perugia's celebrations are as captivating as its history and art. Throughout the year, the city hosts lively festivals and events that showcase its local traditions, including the world-famous Umbria Jazz Festival, which attracts music enthusiasts from all corners of the globe.

Welcome to Perugia, where time-honored architecture, artistic treasures, and warm hospitality combine to create an unforgettable experience. Whether you're an avid history buff, an art aficionado, or a traveler seeking authentic Italian culture, Perugia promises to leave an indelible mark on your heart. Embrace the serenity of its ancient past, the vibrancy of its present, and the promise of countless new memories waiting to be made in this enchanting city of timeless charm.

About the Region: Umbria's Enchanting Tapestry

Nestled at the heart of Italy, the region of Umbria unfurls like an enchanting tapestry, captivating all who venture into its embrace. Known as the "Green Heart of Italy," this picturesque region is a treasure trove of natural beauty, rich history, and profound cultural heritage.

With its rolling hills adorned with olive groves, vineyards, and sunflower fields, Umbria's landscape is a mesmerizing fusion of colors and textures. The timeless charm of its small medieval villages, perched atop hills like sentinels of the past, transports visitors to a bygone era of serenity and simplicity.

Umbria's allure extends beyond its bucolic scenery. As you explore its winding lanes and cobblestone streets, the region's vibrant past comes alive. The Etruscans, the ancient inhabitants of these lands, have left an indelible mark on Umbria's history, and their legacy can be discovered in the intriguing archaeological sites scattered across the region.

Medieval towns and cities, each with its own unique character, offer a glimpse into a world untouched by time. Assisi, the birthplace of St. Francis, exudes an aura of spiritual tranquility as the magnificent Basilica di San Francesco majestically crowns the town's skyline. Spoleto enchants with its imposing fortress and ancient Roman aqueduct, while Gubbio captivates with its perfectly preserved medieval streets and the grandeur of the Palazzo dei Consoli.

Art and culture thrive in Umbria, as evidenced by its countless museums, galleries, and churches adorned with frescoes and masterpieces. The region's artistic legacy shines brightly in Perugia, the bustling capital, where the Galleria Nazionale dell'Umbria houses a treasure trove of artistic wonders from the Renaissance period.

Umbria's culinary traditions are equally enticing. The region's gastronomy reflects a harmonious blend of rustic simplicity and flavorful abundance. Indulge in savory dishes like wild boar ragù, black truffle pasta, and hearty bean soups, paired with locally produced wines that dance on the palate.

But Umbria isn't just about immersing yourself in history and indulging in culinary delights. The region offers a plethora of outdoor adventures, beckoning nature lovers and thrill-seekers alike. From hiking the verdant trails of Mount Subasio to sailing on Lake Trasimeno, there are a myriad of ways to embrace the great outdoors.

Yet, despite its undeniable allure, Umbria remains blissfully undiscovered by the tourist crowds. It retains an authentic charm, where encounters with locals are met with genuine warmth and hospitality, allowing you to experience the region at its most authentic.

Umbria is a place where time slows down, allowing you to savor each moment and bask in the simple pleasures of life. It's a region that embraces you like an old friend, inviting you to delve deeper into its secrets and stories and to become a part of its enchanting tapestry that weaves together the past and the present. Whether you seek tranquility, adventure, or a glimpse into Italy's timeless soul, Umbria stands ready to welcome you with open arms and an invitation to create memories that will last a lifetime.

Unveiling the Irresistible Allure of Perugia

Perugia, a city steeped in history and brimming with captivating charm, beckons travelers from all corners of the world. There are countless reasons why visiting Perugia should be on every traveler's bucket list. Here are some of the irresistible allurements that await you in this enchanting Italian gem.

Perugia's roots trace back to the ancient Etruscan civilization, and its historical significance is evident in the well-preserved architectural gems that grace the city. From the Etruscan Arch and the underground city to the majestic Rocca Paolina, every corner of Perugia tells a story of its rich past.

As the birthplace of renowned artists like Perugino and Raphael, Perugia is a haven for art enthusiasts. The Galleria Nazionale dell'Umbria houses a stunning collection of Italian Renaissance art, including works by these legendary masters, offering an immersive journey through Italy's artistic legacy.

Perugia's vibrant cultural scene is a testament to its young and dynamic population. The city's prestigious University for Foreigners and University of Perugia infuse the atmosphere with youthful energy, adding a cosmopolitan vibe that enriches the experience for visitors.

Wander through the labyrinthine streets of Perugia's historic center, and you'll be captivated by the intricate medieval architecture. The grandeur of the Perugia Cathedral (Cattedrale di

San Lorenzo), the awe-inspiring Fontana Maggiore, and the charming squares create a fairytale-like ambiance.

Umbria's cuisine is a delightful discovery for food lovers. Perugia's culinary scene is a delicious fusion of traditional Italian flavors, and the region is renowned for its olive oil, truffles, and outstanding wines. Savoring the local delicacies in quaint trattorias is an experience not to be missed.

Perugia hosts an array of lively festivals and events throughout the year. The Umbria Jazz Festival, one of Europe's most celebrated music events, draws international jazz enthusiasts, while the Eurochocolate Festival indulges chocolate lovers with a mouthwatering array of treats.

Perched atop a hill, Perugia offers breathtaking panoramic views of the surrounding Umbrian countryside. Whether you're exploring the city's historic walls or venturing to viewpoints like Giardini Carducci, you'll be rewarded with vistas that inspire awe.

While Perugia offers a wealth of attractions, it remains relatively unexplored by the tourist masses. This creates a warm and welcoming atmosphere where you can immerse yourself in authentic Italian culture and forge genuine connections with the locals.

Perugia's central location in Umbria makes it an ideal base for exploring the region's other treasures. Day trips to nearby towns like Assisi, Gubbio, and Spoleto are easily accessible, allowing you to experience more of Umbria's beauty.

Perhaps the most compelling reason to visit Perugia is the sense of timelessness that envelops you as you traverse its streets and squares. The city's ability to seamlessly blend its storied past with modern life creates an unforgettable ambiance that lingers in your heart long after you depart.

Intriguing, historic, and brimming with art and culture, Perugia beckons with a magnetism that is hard to resist. Whether you're a history enthusiast, an art lover, a food connoisseur, or simply seeking an authentic Italian experience, Perugia welcomes you with open arms and promises to leave an indelible mark on your soul.

Chapter 2: Getting Ready for Your Trip

Travel Planning Tips for an Unforgettable Perugia Experience

- **Choose the Right Time to Visit**: Perugia's charm is ever-present, but certain times of the year offer unique experiences. Consider visiting during the spring (April to June) or autumn (September to November), when the weather is pleasant and the tourist crowds are relatively thinner.

- **Research and Itinerary**: Familiarize yourself with Perugia's top attractions, events, and festivals. Create a flexible itinerary to ensure you make the most of your time while leaving room for spontaneous exploration.

- **Accommodation Booking**: Secure your accommodation well in advance, especially during peak seasons or major events. Perugia offers a range of accommodations, from charming boutique hotels to budget-friendly hostels and agriturismos in the countryside.

- **Pack Smartly**: Pack comfortable walking shoes, as exploring Perugia often involves navigating its hilly terrain. Don't forget to bring appropriate attire for the season, and consider packing a reusable water bottle to stay hydrated while sightseeing.

- **Travel Documents and Insurance**: Check visa requirements and ensure your passport is valid for the duration of your trip. Consider purchasing travel insurance to protect yourself from unexpected events.

- **Learn Some Italian**: While many locals in Perugia speak English, knowing a few basic Italian phrases can go a long way in fostering positive interactions with locals and immersing yourself in the local culture.

- **Budget Wisely**: Set a budget for your trip and research average costs for accommodation, meals, and attractions. Keep in mind that many museums and attractions offer discounted tickets for students, seniors, or families.

- **Public Transportation and Parking**: Perugia's historic center is largely pedestrian-friendly, so exploring on foot is a great option. However, if you plan to rent a car, research parking options in advance, as parking in the historic center can be limited.

- **Local Cuisine Exploration**: Perugia's gastronomy is a highlight of any visit. Be adventurous and try local specialties, including truffle dishes, Umbrian salami, and, of course, gelato!

- **Respect Local Customs**: Embrace the local customs and traditions, such as greeting with "buongiorno" (good morning) and "buonasera" (good evening), and remember that mealtimes in Italy are often later than in some other countries.

- **Stay Safe**: Perugia is generally a safe city, but it's always wise to exercise caution with your belongings, especially in crowded areas and on public transportation.

- **Immerse in the Local Culture**: Engage with locals, attend cultural events, and explore beyond the main tourist areas. This will offer a deeper understanding of Perugia's authentic charm.

- **Capture the Moments**: Bring a camera or smartphone to capture the beautiful scenery, stunning architecture, and memorable experiences during your journey.

The Best Time to Embark on a Peruvian Adventure: A Personal Perspective

As someone who fell head over heels for Perugia's enchanting allure, I can't help but share my personal insights on the best time to experience this magical city. Each season in Perugia offers a distinct and captivating charm, making it a year-round destination for travelers seeking a taste of authentic Italy.

Spring: Embrace the Blossoming Beauty

For me, spring is an absolute gem in Perugia. As the days grow longer and the warmth of the sun caresses the hills of Umbria, the city comes alive with a burst of color and energy. The cobbled streets are adorned with blooming flowers, creating a picturesque backdrop for every step you take. The pleasant weather makes it ideal for strolling through the historic center, leisurely exploring every corner, and stumbling upon hidden gems tucked away in charming alleyways.

The city's vibrant cultural scene flourishes during the spring, with numerous festivals and events celebrating music, art, and local traditions. It's a time when you can truly immerse yourself in the essence of Perugia's heritage, as the locals take pride in showcasing their customs with open arms.

Summer: Bask in the Warmth and Festivities
If you're a lover of long, sunny days and a lively atmosphere, summer in Perugia will captivate your heart. While the city does experience an increase in tourists, the vibrant energy and

buzzing streets create an exhilarating ambiance. The Piazza IV Novembre becomes a gathering place for locals and visitors alike, with live performances, open-air concerts, and the jovial spirit of summertime festivities.

The warm weather also allows for excursions to the nearby Lake Trasimeno or the refreshing green landscapes of the surrounding countryside. Whether you're exploring historic sites, indulging in local delicacies, or simply sipping an Aperol Spritz at a lively outdoor cafe, summer in Perugia promises moments of joy and camaraderie.

Autumn: A Tapestry of Colors and Culinary Delights

As the heat of summer subsides, Perugia dons an autumnal cloak of rich, golden hues. The landscape transforms into a breathtaking canvas of colors, with vineyards and olive groves setting the hills ablaze with their amber foliage. The mellow weather invites leisurely walks through the picturesque countryside, where the earthy scent of truffles permeates the air.

Autumn is also a time of gastronomic indulgence in Perugia. The annual Eurochocolate Festival is a paradise for chocolate enthusiasts, offering an array of delectable treats that ignite the senses. Pair this with the harvest season's abundance of local produce, and you have the perfect recipe for a culinary adventure.

Winter: Embrace Cozy Traditions and a Festive Spirit

While winter in Perugia may be colder, it warms the soul with its cozy ambiance and festive traditions. The historic center is adorned with twinkling lights and Christmas markets, exuding a charming yuletide atmosphere. Sip on mulled wine, savor roasted chestnuts, and explore the stalls of handcrafted gifts, immersing yourself in the heartwarming spirit of the season.

Winter is also an excellent time to visit museums and art galleries, where you can appreciate the region's artistic legacy without the summer crowds. The quieter streets lend themselves to intimate experiences, whether you're admiring Renaissance masterpieces or savoring hearty Umbrian dishes in the comfort of a welcoming trattoria.

Ultimately, the best time to visit Perugia is a deeply personal choice, influenced by your preferences and what you wish to experience. Whether you choose to embrace the blooming beauty of spring, the festive warmth of summer, the tapestry of colors in autumn, or the cozy traditions of winter, Perugia will embrace you with its timeless charm and leave you with cherished memories that will stay with you forever.

Visa and Entry Requirements

As of my last update in September 2021, here are some general guidelines regarding visa and entry requirements for visiting Italy, including Perugia. However, please note that immigration policies can change, so it's essential to verify the latest information with the Italian embassy or consulate in your country before planning your trip.

- **Schengen Area and EU Countries**: Italy is a member of the Schengen Area, which is a group of European countries that have abolished internal border controls. If you are a citizen of a Schengen Area country or another European Union (EU) member state, you can travel to Italy and stay for up to 90 days without a visa.

- **Visa-Free Entry for Certain Nationalities**: Citizens of certain countries, including the United States, Canada, Australia, New Zealand, Japan, South Korea, and many others, can enter Italy and the Schengen Area for tourist purposes without a visa for up to 90 days within a 180-day period. This is for short-term stays, such as tourism, business meetings, or visiting family and friends.

- **Schengen Visa**: If you are a citizen of a country that is not visa-exempt, you will need to apply for a Schengen visa from the Italian embassy or consulate in your home country. The Schengen visa allows you to enter the Schengen Area, which includes Italy, for up to 90 days within a

180-day period for tourism, business, or family visits.

- **Long-Term Stays**: If you plan to stay in Italy and the Schengen Area for longer than 90 days or for purposes other than tourism, you may need to apply for a national visa or residence permit, depending on the purpose of your stay. These visas are usually required for work, study, family reunification, or other extended stays.

- **Passport Requirements**: Regardless of whether you need a visa or not, all travelers must have a valid passport with at least six months of validity beyond their planned stay in Italy.

Transportation Options

Transportation in Perugia and the surrounding areas offers a mix of convenience, scenic routes, and various choices to suit different travel preferences. Here are the primary transportation options to consider when exploring Perugia:

- **Walking**: Perugia's historic center is best explored on foot. The city's compact size and pedestrian-friendly streets make walking an ideal way to soak in the charming atmosphere, discover hidden corners, and easily access major landmarks.

- **Public Transportation**: Perugia has an efficient public transportation system, which includes buses and a mini-metro (a small-scale automated light rail system). Buses connect various parts of the city, including the historic center, train station, and surrounding neighborhoods. The mini-metro links the city center with the Pian di Massiano area and provides a convenient and scenic route.

- **Taxis and Rideshare Services**: Taxis are available throughout Perugia, and they are a convenient option for getting around the city and to nearby destinations. Additionally, rideshare services like Uber are also available in some areas, providing another flexible transportation choice.

- **Renting a Car**: If you plan to explore the beautiful countryside and nearby towns in Umbria, renting a car can be a great option. Having a car gives you the freedom to venture beyond the city and visit charming villages, scenic landscapes, and other attractions at your own pace.

- **Bicycles and Scooters**: Perugia offers bicycle rental services, and cycling can be a fun and eco-friendly way to explore the city and its surroundings. Additionally, some areas may offer scooter rental options for shorter trips or sightseeing.

- **Trains**: Perugia is connected to other major Italian cities and regions by the national train network. The Perugia train station, known as Perugia Fontivegge, serves as a gateway to the city, and frequent trains run to and from destinations like Rome, Florence, and other cities in Italy.

- **Day Tours and Excursions**: Many tour operators offer guided day tours and excursions from Perugia to nearby towns and attractions. These tours can be a convenient way to explore the region without the hassle of planning logistics.

Before choosing a transportation option, consider factors like your itinerary, the places you want to visit, your budget, and your preferences for convenience and flexibility. Perugia's mix of transportation choices ensures that you can navigate the city and its surroundings with ease, allowing you to make the most of your travel experience.

Chapter 3: Perugia Travel Itineraries

One Day in Perugia: An Unforgettable Journey through History, Art, and Gastronomy

Morning

As the sun gently rises over the picturesque hills of Umbria, begin your day in the heart of Perugia's historic center. Wander through the cobblestone streets and narrow alleyways, where every step unveils the city's rich history and timeless charm. Start at Piazza IV Novembre, the bustling hub of Perugia, and marvel at the stunning Fontana Maggiore, an intricate medieval fountain adorned with allegorical sculptures.

Immerse yourself in the grandeur of the Perugia Cathedral, Cattedrale di San Lorenzo, with its Gothic façade and awe-inspiring interiors. Continue your exploration at Palazzo dei Priori, a majestic medieval palace housing the city's town hall and an art gallery showcasing works by renowned Italian artists.

Don't miss the opportunity to explore Perugia's underground city, a labyrinth of ancient Etruscan passageways and medieval cellars that offer a glimpse into the city's hidden past. You can join a guided tour or venture on your own, discovering the secrets that lie beneath the surface.

Afternoon

As the sun climbs higher, delve deeper into Perugia's artistic heritage. Head to the Galleria

Nazionale dell'Umbria, a treasure trove of Italian Renaissance art located within the Palazzo dei Priori. Admire masterpieces by Perugino, Pinturicchio, and Raphael, as well as other works that reflect the region's artistic legacy.

Stroll through the charming streets to find unique art galleries and artisan workshops, where you can witness local artists at work and purchase one-of-a-kind souvenirs.

For a dose of history and culture, visit the Etruscan Arch and the remaining sections of Perugia's ancient city walls. These ancient structures offer a glimpse into Perugia's origins and showcase the city's resilience throughout the ages.

Evening

As the day draws to a close, head to one of Perugia's panoramic viewpoints to witness a breathtaking sunset over the rolling Umbrian hills. Giardini Carducci, located near the city center, provides an idyllic spot to savor the mesmerizing hues as the sun dips below the horizon.

For a memorable dining experience, venture into one of Perugia's cozy trattorias or family-run restaurants. Indulge in traditional Umbrian dishes, such as strangozzi pasta with truffle sauce or a hearty wild boar stew. Pair your meal with a fine local wine, and don't forget to leave room for a delightful dessert, such as torta al testo or tiramisu.

As the evening unfolds, wander through the illuminated streets of Perugia's historic center, taking in the enchanting ambiance and lively atmosphere. Visit a gelateria to savor a scoop of authentic Italian gelato or sip on a fragrant espresso at a local café, savoring the final moments of your day in Perugia.

One day in Perugia may seem fleeting, but this journey through history, art, and gastronomy will leave an indelible mark on your heart. Embrace the city's timeless charm, relish in its artistic wonders, and savor the flavors of Umbria, creating cherished memories that will linger in your soul for years to come.

Two Days in Perugia: A Delightful Exploration of Architecture, Markets, and Wine

Day 1: Perugia's Architectural Gems

Morning

Begin your first day in Perugia with a deep dive into the city's architectural treasures. Start at Piazza IV Novembre, where the elegant Fontana Maggiore takes center stage. Admire the intricate sculptures and reliefs that adorn this medieval masterpiece. Just a short walk away, the Perugia Cathedral, Cattedrale di San Lorenzo, awaits with its grand Gothic façade and stunning artworks inside.

Tip: Climb the Cathedral's bell tower for panoramic views of Perugia and the surrounding landscapes.

Next, venture into the Palazzo dei Priori, a striking medieval palace housing the town hall and an impressive art gallery. Marvel at masterpieces by Perugino, Pinturicchio, and Raphael, among others, as you immerse yourself in the richness of Italian Renaissance art.

Afternoon

Indulge in a leisurely lunch at one of Perugia's charming trattorias, savoring regional delicacies and local wines. Afterward, take a guided tour or venture on your own to explore Perugia's fascinating underground city. Wander through ancient Etruscan passages and medieval cellars, discovering the mysteries hidden beneath the bustling streets.

Evening

As the day winds down, embrace the romantic atmosphere of Perugia's historic center. Take an evening passeggiata (stroll) through the illuminated streets, and perhaps join the locals for an aperitivo at one of the trendy bars. Enjoy a refreshing Spritz or a glass of Prosecco while soaking in the enchanting ambiance.

Day 2: Local Markets and Wine Tasting

Morning

On your second day, venture beyond the city center to experience Perugia's vibrant local markets. Visit the Mercato Coperto, a lively indoor market brimming with fresh produce, cheeses, meats, and artisanal products. Engage with friendly vendors, taste some regional specialties, and perhaps pick up some picnic supplies for later.

Tip: Try porchetta, a succulent roasted pork dish, and indulge in the myriad of flavorful cheeses from the region.

Afternoon

In the afternoon, venture into the picturesque Umbrian countryside for a delightful wine-tasting experience. Several wineries in the surrounding areas offer tours and tastings, allowing you to savor the diverse flavors of Umbrian wines, such as Sagrantino, Grechetto, and Sangiovese. Enjoy the scenic vineyard views and learn about the winemaking process directly from passionate local vintners.

Evening

Return to Perugia and find a cozy spot for a memorable dinner. Many restaurants in the city showcase the bounty of Umbria's local ingredients in their dishes. Relish the flavors of freshly made pasta, truffle-infused delicacies, and delectable desserts while toasting to the joys of your Peruvian adventure.

As you bid farewell to Perugia, you'll carry with you a trove of cherished memories, from the awe-inspiring architectural wonders to the bustling markets and the soulful sips of wine. Embrace the essence of this charming city, and let the magic of Perugia linger in your heart for years to come.

Three Days in Perugia and Beyond: Unveiling the Treasures of Perugia and Umbria

Day 1: Perugia City Tour

Morning

Embark on a comprehensive city tour of Perugia, starting with a visit to the magnificent Piazza IV Novembre. Marvel at the intricacies of the Fontana Maggiore and soak in the historical ambiance of this bustling square. Head to the Perugia Cathedral, Cattedrale di San Lorenzo, to admire its Gothic beauty and explore its art-filled interiors.

Tip: Climb the cathedral's bell tower for panoramic views over Perugia and the rolling Umbrian hills.

Next, explore the Palazzo dei Priori, where you can immerse yourself in the region's artistic heritage at the Galleria Nazionale dell'Umbria. Witness masterpieces by Perugino, Pinturicchio, and other Italian Renaissance artists, gaining insight into the city's artistic legacy.

.

Afternoon

After a delightful lunch in a local trattoria, venture into Perugia's underground city. Uncover the secrets of ancient Etruscan passageways and medieval cellars, gaining a unique perspective on the city's history and evolution.

Evening

As evening descends, take a leisurely passeggiata through Perugia's illuminated streets. Savor an aperitivo at one of the chic bars and indulge in the city's vibrant nightlife. Find a cozy restaurant to relish traditional Umbrian dishes paired with local wines, culminating your first day in Perugia with a memorable dining experience.

Day 2: A Day Trip to Assisi

Morning

Embark on an enchanting day trip to Assisi, a UNESCO World Heritage Site and a spiritual gem of Umbria. Upon arrival, visit the stunning Basilica di San Francesco, the final resting place of St. Francis of Assisi. Admire the frescoes by Giotto and Cimabue, which narrate the life of this beloved saint.

Afternoon

Stroll through the charming streets of Assisi, where time seems to stand still. Explore the medieval alleys, visit the Roman Temple of Minerva, and savor the panoramic views over the Umbrian landscape from the Rocca Maggiore fortress.

Tip: Treat yourself to some Assisi chocolate, a local specialty produced by the town's chocolatiers.

Day 3: Exploring Umbria's Countryside

Morning

On your third day, set out to explore the picturesque Umbrian countryside. Drive or join a guided tour to visit the beautiful Lake Trasimeno, the largest lake in central Italy. Enjoy a relaxing boat ride or stroll along the lake's shores, absorbing the tranquility of the surroundings.

Afternoon

Continue your countryside exploration with a visit to one of the charming villages scattered across the region. Consider stops in Gubbio, with its medieval charm and Palazzo dei Consoli, or Spoleto, home to the magnificent Ponte delle Torri and the beautiful Duomo.

Evening

As the day comes to a close, return to Perugia and perhaps take one last evening stroll through the city's vibrant streets. Savor a farewell dinner at a beloved local eatery, reflecting on the memories made during your unforgettable three-day journey through Perugia and beyond.

From Perugia's architectural marvels to the spiritual sanctity of Assisi and the natural beauty of Umbria's countryside, this three-day itinerary unveils the diverse and captivating facets of this enchanting region. Embrace the history, art, and serenity that Umbria offers, creating cherished memories that will linger in your heart for a lifetime.

Chapter 4: Top Attractions and Things to Do

Piazza IV Novembre and the Fontana Maggiore: The Heart of Perugia's Timeless Charm

Piazza IV Novembre stands as the vibrant heart of Perugia, a bustling square that encapsulates the city's rich history and enduring allure. Nestled within the charming maze of narrow streets in the historic center, this enchanting square has been the center of social, religious, and cultural life in Perugia for centuries.

At the heart of Piazza IV Novembre stands the Fontana Maggiore, a magnificent and elaborate medieval fountain that serves as the centerpiece of the square. The Fontana Maggiore, crafted by the talented sculptors Nicola and Giovanni Pisano between 1275 and 1278, is a masterpiece of Gothic artistry and architectural ingenuity.

The fountain's name, "Fontana Maggiore," translates to "The Major Fountain," and it truly lives up to its grand title. With its awe-inspiring dimensions and intricate details, the fountain is a captivating sight that beckons visitors and locals alike.

The Fontana Maggiore is a triple-tiered structure adorned with exquisite bas-reliefs, statues, and ornamental carvings. The lower basin features 50 sculpted panels that depict various allegorical and historical scenes, ranging from biblical stories to representations of the months and the liberal arts. Each panel tells a unique tale, inviting viewers to unravel the stories etched into the stone.

The second tier showcases 24 statues of prophets, saints, and mythological figures, offering a striking display of craftsmanship. Crowning the fountain is a majestic bronze statue of a griffin, the symbol of Perugia, which adds an air of majesty to the entire structure.

Beyond its artistic splendor, the Fontana Maggiore served practical purposes as well. It provided the city with a reliable water supply during medieval times, a vital resource in an era when water scarcity was a constant concern.

Over the centuries, Piazza IV Novembre and the Fontana Maggiore have witnessed countless historical events, festivals, and gatherings. The square has been a witness to joyous celebrations, solemn processions, and the ebb and flow of daily life in Perugia.

Today, Piazza IV Novembre continues to be a vibrant hub where locals and visitors converge. Cafés and restaurants encircle the square, offering perfect vantage points to admire the fountain and absorb the lively atmosphere. From morning until late at night, the square remains alive with the buzz of conversation, the laughter of children, and the footsteps of passersby.

For those visiting Perugia, Piazza IV Novembre and the Fontana Maggiore are essential stops on the itinerary. Take a moment to bask in the fountain's intricate beauty and let the history and artistry of this iconic square transport you back in time. As you sit amidst the echoes of the past, you will find yourself enveloped in Perugia's timeless charm, creating memories that will forever resonate in your heart.

Perugia Cathedral (Cattedrale di San Lorenzo): A Majestic Marvel of Gothic Architecture

Perched atop the hill of Perugia, the Cattedrale di San Lorenzo, also known as Perugia Cathedral, stands as a symbol of the city's religious significance and architectural splendor. With its majestic façade and awe-inspiring interiors, the cathedral has been a spiritual and cultural landmark for centuries, attracting visitors from near and far.

The origins of Perugia Cathedral date back to the 10th century, when it was originally built as a Romanesque church. Over the centuries, the cathedral underwent several renovations and expansions, eventually taking on the magnificent Gothic style that we see today.

Approaching the cathedral, visitors are immediately drawn to the impressive façade, adorned with intricate decorations and sculptures. The central rose window, surrounded by delicate Gothic tracery, mesmerizes with its ethereal beauty. The façade's three ornate doorways feature a wealth of religious motifs, telling stories of saints, biblical events, and heavenly visions.

Once inside, visitors are greeted by a sense of grandeur that befits a place of worship as significant as Perugia Cathedral. The interior is characterized by soaring arches, rib-vaulted ceilings, and an abundance of colorful stained glass windows that flood the space with a kaleidoscope of light.

One of the most treasured artistic masterpieces housed within the cathedral is the "Martyrdom of Saint Lawrence," a stunning fresco painted by Pietro Perugino in the 16th century. This masterpiece graces the Cappella di San Lorenzo, adding to the spiritual and artistic allure of the cathedral.

Another notable feature of the cathedral is its beautifully carved wooden choir stalls, a testament to the craftsmanship of the Renaissance artisans. These intricately designed stalls offer a glimpse into the religious and artistic fervor that characterized the Renaissance era.

For those with an adventurous spirit, climbing the bell tower of Perugia Cathedral presents an opportunity for breathtaking panoramic views of the city and the surrounding countryside. The climb is rewarded with a captivating vista that showcases the beauty of Perugia from above.

Throughout the year, the cathedral hosts religious ceremonies, concerts, and cultural events that further enrich the spiritual and artistic atmosphere of this hallowed space.

As you step out of Perugia Cathedral, you can't help but marvel at the intricate beauty and historical significance of this Gothic gem. Whether you are an art enthusiast, a history lover, or a seeker of spiritual tranquility, a visit to Perugia Cathedral promises a journey through time and an unforgettable experience of Italy's artistic and religious heritage.

Rocca Paolina: Unraveling the History of Perugia's Fortified Citadel

Rocca Paolina stands as a powerful testament to Perugia's complex and tumultuous past, offering visitors a fascinating journey through the city's history and architecture. This imposing fortress, located at the heart of the historic center, is a remnant of a bygone era, serving as a poignant reminder of both the city's strength and the forces that once sought to control it.

The origins of Rocca Paolina can be traced back to the mid-16th century, when Pope Paul III, seeking to assert his authority over Perugia, ordered the construction of this formidable citadel. The fortress was strategically built atop the ruins of the medieval district, known as the

"Borgo," which had been famously rebellious against papal rule.

Rocca Paolina served not only as a symbol of papal power but also as a means of suppressing any opposition from the citizens of Perugia. The massive structure boasted thick walls, imposing gates, and underground passages, creating an intimidating presence that loomed over the city.

Over the years, the fortress underwent various modifications, expanding and incorporating the existing buildings of the Borgo into its structure. As a result, the original medieval neighborhood was engulfed within the walls of the Rocca, leading to the displacement of its inhabitants and the radical transformation of the area.

The history of Rocca Paolina took a dramatic turn in the 19th century when the Papal States fell and Italy unified into a single nation. As a symbolic act of liberation, the citizens of Perugia tore down the oppressive walls of the fortress, demolishing the exterior that had dominated the city for centuries.

However, the story of Rocca Paolina does not end there. Today, the remains of the fortress have been partially excavated and preserved, creating an intriguing underground city that offers visitors a glimpse into the past. The underground passages, cellars, and archways that once lay hidden beneath the imposing structure are now open for exploration, revealing the hidden layers of Perugia's history.

Visitors can descend into this subterranean world and explore the fascinating network of rooms and corridors. The underground site hosts art exhibitions, cultural events, and historical displays that add to the allure of this unique archaeological site.

Rocca Paolina has transformed from a symbol of oppression to a living testament of Perugia's resilience and determination to preserve its identity and heritage. The site serves as a poignant reminder of the complexities of history and the enduring spirit of a city that has weathered the storms of time.

For those who venture into the depths of Rocca Paolina, the experience is both educational and evocative. It is a journey that offers a profound understanding of the forces that have shaped

Perugia's past and a renewed appreciation for the city's enduring spirit and cultural richness.

Galleria Nazionale dell'Umbria: A Captivating Journey Through Umbria's Artistic Heritage

Nestled within the magnificent Palazzo dei Priori in Perugia, the Galleria Nazionale dell'Umbria (National Gallery of Umbria) is a treasure trove of artistic masterpieces that offers a captivating journey through the rich cultural heritage of the Umbria region. This art gallery stands as a testament to the artistic brilliance that flourished in Umbria, showcasing the works of renowned artists that span various periods and styles.

The Galleria Nazionale dell'Umbria houses an extensive collection of paintings, sculptures, illuminated manuscripts, and decorative arts, which provide a comprehensive overview of

Umbria's artistic legacy. The gallery's collection dates back to the Middle Ages, encompassing works from the Byzantine, Gothic, Renaissance, and Baroque eras, as well as later periods.

As you enter the gallery, you are immediately immersed in the artistic richness that defines Umbria's contribution to the Italian art scene. The grand halls and majestic rooms of Palazzo dei Priori create a fitting backdrop for the impressive array of artworks on display.

One of the highlights of the gallery is the collection of paintings by the renowned Umbrian artist Pietro Perugino. His delicate brushwork and luminous colors are showcased in masterpieces such as "The Ascension of Christ" and "The Adoration of the Magi," providing a glimpse into the artistic genius of this celebrated painter.

The Galleria Nazionale dell'Umbria also boasts works by other prominent artists, including Pinturicchio, Benedetto Bonfigli, and Luca Signorelli, among others. Each painting offers a unique perspective on religious themes, historical events, and the daily life of the people of Umbria, providing a window into the region's cultural and social history.

Aside from paintings, the gallery houses an impressive collection of sculptures, including medieval and Renaissance sculptures crafted by skilled Umbrian artists. These sculptures add a three-dimensional dimension to the artistic journey, further enriching the visitor's experience.

Visiting the Galleria Nazionale dell'Umbria is not only an opportunity to admire individual artworks but also to witness the evolution of artistic styles and techniques over the centuries. From the solemn and contemplative art of the Middle Ages to the exuberance of the Renaissance and the emotional intensity of the Baroque period, the gallery offers a comprehensive survey of Umbria's artistic heritage.

As you explore the Galleria Nazionale dell'Umbria, you can't help but be captivated by the sheer talent and creativity of the artists who shaped the region's cultural identity. The gallery's collection provides a profound appreciation for the artistic legacy that Umbria has bequeathed to the world, making it a must-visit destination for art enthusiasts and history lovers alike.

The Etruscan Arch and City Walls: Ancient Remnants of Perugia's Past

As you wander through the historic center of Perugia, you may stumble upon two fascinating vestiges of the city's ancient past: the Etruscan Arch and the remnants of the city walls. These ancient structures serve as tangible links to Perugia's Etruscan origins, providing a glimpse into the city's early history and the civilizations that once thrived within its walls.

The Etruscan Arch, also known as the Arch of Augustus, is a magnificent gateway that stands as a tribute to the engineering prowess of the Etruscan civilization. Dating back to the 3rd century BC, this arch is one of the best-preserved Etruscan structures in Perugia.

As you approach the arch, you are immediately struck by its grandeur and historical significance. The arch's construction features massive travertine blocks held together without the use of mortar, a testament to the architectural expertise of the Etruscans. It once served as a fortified entrance to the city, allowing access through the Etruscan walls that encircled Perugia.

The Etruscan Arch is adorned with inscriptions and symbols, including the Latin dedication to Emperor Augustus, who rebuilt the arch in the 1st century BC. This inscription serves as a testament to the arch's continuous importance throughout the ages and its association with significant historical events.

As you explore Perugia, you may notice traces of the ancient city walls that once encircled the city, marking its boundaries and providing protection from potential invaders. The Etruscans originally constructed these walls during the 3rd and 4th centuries BC, and they were later expanded and fortified by the Romans, medieval rulers, and subsequent civilizations.

The city walls were essential for safeguarding Perugia's inhabitants, fortifying the city against external threats, and asserting its prominence as a regional power. Over the centuries, the walls were enhanced with defensive towers, gates, and bastions, each addition reflecting the strategic considerations of the era.

While much of the original city wall has been incorporated into the fabric of the modern city, some sections are still visible, reminding visitors of the ancient boundaries that shaped Perugia's growth and development.

Today, the Etruscan Arch and the remnants of the city walls stand as reminders of the city's storied past, and they offer a unique opportunity to connect with the ancient civilizations that once called Perugia home. As you walk through these historic structures, you can't help but marvel at the ingenuity and artistry of the Etruscans and their lasting impact on the city's identity. They stand as silent witnesses to the passage of time and the continuity of life in Perugia, inviting visitors to embrace the city's historical tapestry and immerse themselves in its timeless charm.

A Sweet Delight: Perugina Chocolate Factory Tour

For chocolate enthusiasts and curious travelers alike, the Perugina Chocolate Factory Tour is a delectable experience that offers a behind-the-scenes glimpse into the world of one of Italy's most iconic chocolatiers. Founded in 1907, Perugina has become synonymous with high-quality chocolates, including their famous Baci (Kisses), small chocolate pralines filled with a velvety hazelnut center and wrapped in a love note.

The tour begins with a warm welcome at the Perugina Chocolate Factory, located just a short distance from the historic center of Perugia. Upon arrival, you'll be greeted by the sweet aroma of chocolate that permeates the air, setting the stage for a delightful and immersive experience.

An expert guide will lead you through the various stages of chocolate production, providing fascinating insights into the chocolate-making process. You'll learn about the sourcing of the finest cocoa beans, the meticulous roasting and grinding, and the delicate blending of ingredients to achieve the perfect flavor and texture.

Of course, the highlight of the tour is discovering the secrets behind Perugino's beloved Baci chocolates. Witness skilled chocolatiers as they meticulously mold, fill, and wrap each Baci with care and precision. You'll gain a deeper appreciation for the craftsmanship and dedication that go into creating these iconic confections.

As the tour progresses, you'll have the opportunity to indulge in generous tastings of Perugino's various chocolate creations. Savor the velvety richness of different chocolate blends and delight in the harmonious pairing of chocolate and hazelnuts in the Baci pralines.

For those with a creative flair, you can also try your hand at personalizing your own Baci love notes, adding a personal touch to these sweet expressions of affection.

Before concluding the tour, don't forget to visit the factory's charming gift shop, where you can stock up on a wide array of Perugina chocolates and chocolate-related products. It's the perfect place to pick up delectable souvenirs for loved ones back home or simply to treat yourself to more of the irresistible sweetness.

Booking and Practical Information

To ensure availability and avoid disappointment, it's recommended to book the Perugina Chocolate Factory Tour in advance, especially during peak tourist seasons. The tour typically lasts for about an hour, but the memories and the taste of Perugino's exquisite chocolates will linger long after the tour is over.

The Perugina Chocolate Factory Tour offers a delightful journey through the world of chocolate, allowing visitors to witness the magic behind these delectable treats. It's a must-do experience for anyone visiting Perugia, whether you are a devoted chocolate lover or simply curious to explore the sweet side of this enchanting city. So, indulge your senses and let the chocolatey delights of Perugina leave a lasting impression on your taste buds and your heart.

Underground Perugia: Unveiling the Hidden Depths of History

Beneath the charming streets and bustling squares of Perugia lies a fascinating world waiting to be explored: Underground Perugia. This subterranean city is a labyrinth of ancient passageways, Etruscan wells, medieval cisterns, and hidden chambers that bear witness to the city's layered history.

Underground Perugia offers a unique perspective on the city's evolution through the ages. The Etruscans, the ancient civilization that predates Rome, first established a network of tunnels and wells beneath the city. These Etruscan passages, known as "Ipogei," served various purposes, from providing water storage to acting as religious sanctuaries.

As you descend into the underground realm, expert guides lead the way, shedding light on the historical significance of each space. You'll meander through narrow passages, illuminated by soft lights that add an air of mystery to the experience.

- Etruscan Wells: One of the highlights of Underground Perugia is the exploration of Etruscan wells. These deep, cylindrical wells were ingeniously constructed to capture and store rainwater, providing a vital water supply for the ancient inhabitants of Perugia. Descending into the wells, you'll marvel at the ingenuity and engineering prowess of the Etruscans, who carved these impressive structures into the rock.

- Medieval Cisterns: During the medieval period, Perugia expanded its underground network with the construction of cisterns. These large underground reservoirs were used to store rainwater and were essential for supporting the city's growing population. The cisterns, with their vaulted ceilings and sturdy pillars, evoke a sense of awe and wonder as you explore their cavernous depths.

- The Baglioni Hypogeum: Another notable site in Underground Perugia is the Baglioni Hypogeum. This secret underground chamber, hidden beneath a seemingly ordinary building, served as a refuge for the Baglioni family during times of political strife in the 16th century.

As you venture into this clandestine space, you'll uncover tales of intrigue, power struggles, and human ingenuity to protect one's family and lineage.

Practical Information

Wear comfortable shoes and be prepared for some uneven surfaces and stairs as you navigate the underground passages. Additionally, make sure to check the tour's operating hours and availability, as they may vary throughout the year.

Underground Perugia offers a captivating journey through time, unraveling the mysteries that lie beneath the surface of this ancient city. With each step into the depths, you'll feel a sense of connection with the past as the echoes of history reverberate through the underground passages. It's a one-of-a-kind experience that allows you to truly immerse yourself in the fascinating layers of Perugia's hidden history, leaving you with lasting memories of this intriguing and enchanting subterranean world.

Chapter 5: Culinary Delights

Umbrian Cuisine: A Gastronomic Journey into the Heart of Italy's Culinary Delights

Umbria, often referred to as the "Green Heart of Italy," not only captivates visitors with its picturesque landscapes but also tempts the taste buds with its rich and flavorful cuisine. This region boasts a gastronomic heritage deeply rooted in tradition, locally sourced ingredients, and time-honored cooking techniques. Embark on a culinary adventure through Umbria, where every dish tells a story and every meal becomes a cherished memory.

- **Truffles**: A Treasure of the Earth Umbria is renowned for its truffles, the elusive and aromatic fungi that add a touch of luxury to the local cuisine. The prized black truffles, particularly the esteemed tartufo nero pregiato, are expertly hunted by skilled truffle hunters and their trusty dogs in the wooded hills of the region. Indulge in truffle-infused dishes such as homemade pasta with truffle sauce, risotto with truffles, or a simple yet sublime truffle-infused omelet. The earthy, intoxicating aroma of truffles will transport you to a realm of pure culinary pleasure.

- **Norcineria**: Cured Meats and Sausages Umbria's Norcineria tradition showcases the art of charcuterie at its finest. Sample a variety of cured meats and sausages, such as prosciutto, salami, and capocollo, which are carefully crafted using time-honored techniques passed down through generations. Pair these delectable meats with local cheeses and a glass of robust Umbrian wine for an authentic Italian antipasto experience.

Legumes and Lentils: Nourishment from the Land

Umbria's fertile lands yield a bounty of nutritious legumes, and lentils, in particular, take center stage in the regional cuisine. Castelluccio di Norcia, a picturesque village in the Umbrian Apennines, is famous for its small, delicate lentils known as "lenticchie di Castelluccio." Savor hearty lentil soups, stews, and salads, each showcasing the simplicity and authenticity of Umbrian farm-to-table fare.

Wild Boar: A Taste of Tradition

In Umbria, wild boar, or "cinghiale," is a beloved ingredient in traditional recipes. From savory stews and hearty ragùs to flavorful sausages, wild boar takes on a starring role in the region's culinary repertoire. The tender and succulent meat is often paired with juniper berries, rosemary, and other aromatic herbs, creating a taste that is both rustic and refined.

Olive Oil: The Liquid Gold of Umbria

Olive oil, the liquid gold of Umbria, is the foundation of many dishes in the region's cuisine. The rolling hills of Umbria are dotted with olive groves that produce some of the finest extra virgin olive oils in Italy. Taste this golden elixir drizzled over bruschetta, salads, or hearty bean soups, and let the smooth and fruity flavors dance on your palate.

Sagrantino Wine: A Toast to Umbrian Hospitality

No gastronomic journey through Umbria is complete without savoring its exceptional wines. Umbria is celebrated for its robust red wines, with Sagrantino being the most prominent. Indulge in the full-bodied and tannic Sagrantino di Montefalco, a wine that perfectly complements the region's hearty dishes. As you raise your glass, you'll discover that every sip embodies the warmth and generosity of Umbrian hospitality.

Dolci: A Sweet Finale

Complete your gastronomic journey with Umbria's delightful dolci (desserts). From the indulgent torciglione, a spiral-shaped pastry filled with almonds and chocolate, to the delicate pampepato, a spiced cake with dried fruit and nuts, Umbria offers a sweet array of treats to satisfy your sweet tooth.

Umbrian cuisine is a celebration of the region's bountiful lands and time-honored traditions. Each dish reflects the passion and pride of the local chefs, who strive to preserve the culinary heritage of this enchanting region. As you embark on this gastronomic journey, you'll find that Umbria not only captures your heart but also leaves an indelible mark on your palate, making your visit truly a feast for the senses.

Must-Try Local Dishes

When visiting Umbria, there are several must-try local dishes and restaurants that will immerse you in the authentic flavors of the region. From traditional Umbrian specialties to innovative culinary creations, these dishes and restaurants promise an unforgettable gastronomic experience. Here are some top recommendations:

1. **Strangozzi al Tartufo**: Indulge in this delectable dish of hand-rolled, thick spaghetti-like pasta, known as strangozzi, dressed with a luxurious truffle sauce made from the region's prized black truffles. This dish captures the essence of Umbria's truffle-rich culinary heritage.

2. **Norcineria Platter**: Enjoy a platter of various cured meats and sausages from Umbria's Norcineria tradition. Savor slices of prosciutto, salami, capocollo, and other cured delights, each highlighting the region's time-honored charcuterie craftsmanship.

3. **Pasta alla Norcina**: This hearty pasta dish features hand-rolled pasta served with a rich and creamy sauce made from fresh pork sausage, truffles, and cream. It is a true comfort food, showcasing the flavors of Norcia, a town renowned for its sausages.

4. **Tagliatelle al Sagrantino**: Experience the marriage of Sagrantino wine and pasta in this dish. Tagliatelle pasta is tossed in a

rich sauce made with the bold and tannic Sagrantino wine, creating a harmonious balance of flavors.

5. **Umbricelli**: Another pasta specialty of Umbria, Umbricelli is a thick, hand-rolled pasta typically served with simple but delicious sauces like tomato and basil or garlic and oil. Its rustic charm and chewy texture make it a favorite among locals.

6. **Cinghiale**: Savor the flavors of wild boar in various dishes, such as wild boar stew, ragù, or sausages. The tender and savory meat pairs perfectly with the aromatic herbs and spices used in Umbrian cuisine.

Must-Try Restaurants

- **Antica Trattoria San Lorenzo (Perugia)**: Located in the heart of Perugia, this historic trattoria serves traditional Umbrian dishes with a focus on seasonal and locally sourced ingredients. Don't miss their truffle-infused pasta dishes and hearty meat specialties.

- **Norcineria IGP (Norcia)**: When in Norcia, a visit to this charming restaurant is a must. They specialize in dishes featuring Norcia's renowned cured meats and sausages, allowing you to taste the best of Umbrian charcuterie.

- **Trattoria di Oscar (Assisi)**: Nestled in the medieval town of Assisi, this trattoria offers a warm and welcoming atmosphere and serves classic Umbrian dishes with a modern twist. Their menu showcases the freshest local produce and flavors.

- **Ristorante Enoteca L'Umbricello (Torgiano)**: This restaurant in the charming town of Torgiano offers an excellent selection of Umbrian wines to accompany their traditional and innovative dishes. Their Umbricelli and truffle dishes are highly recommended.

- **Osteria a Priori (Perugia)**: Situated in a historic building, this osteria exudes rustic charm and serves a delightful array of Umbrian delicacies. From homemade pasta to sumptuous roasts, their menu celebrates the best of Umbrian cuisine.

- **Il Tartufo (Spoleto)**: For a true truffle experience, head to this restaurant in Spoleto. Their truffle-infused dishes, especially their pastas and risottos, are crafted with precision to highlight the unique flavors of Umbria's prized truffles.

Perugia's Coffee Culture: A Ritual of Flavor and Social Bonding

In the heart of Italy, where coffee is not merely a drink but an art form, Perugia stands out as a city with a thriving coffee culture that permeates daily life. From the early morning espresso to the afternoon coffee break, coffee holds a special place in the hearts of Peruvians, serving as both a source of energy and a means of social connection.

- **The Espresso Ritual**: In Perugia, like in many parts of Italy, coffee often begins with the iconic espresso. The compact shot of strong, aromatic coffee is a morning ritual for many locals, setting the tone for the day ahead. Whether it's enjoyed at a bustling café or simply sipped standing at the counter, espresso is a quick but cherished moment to awaken the senses and kickstart the day.

- **Cappuccino and Beyond**: As the morning progresses, Peruvians often indulge in a cappuccino—a velvety blend of espresso and frothy milk. However, it's essential to note that, in Italy, cappuccinos are typically enjoyed only in the morning. After midday, locals prefer to steer clear of milky coffee and opt for other options, such as macchiato (espresso "stained" with a small amount of milk) or caffè lungo (a longer espresso).

- **The Art of Coffee Socializing**: For Peruvians, coffee is not merely about satisfying a caffeine craving; it's a social activity that fosters connections and conversations. Throughout the day, friends and colleagues gather at local coffee bars to engage in lively discussions while sipping their favorite coffee concoctions. The café culture of Perugia encourages community bonding, where people from all walks of life come together over a shared love for coffee and camaraderie.

- **Pasticcerie and Sweet Temptations**: Pairing coffee with delectable pastries is a delightful tradition in Perugia. Pasticcerie, or pastry shops, are havens for those with a sweet tooth. Locals often treat themselves to "pasticciotto," a buttery pastry filled with cream or jam, or "biscotti," crunchy cookies perfect for dipping in coffee. The combination of coffee and pastries elevates the coffee experience, creating a harmonious symphony of flavors.

- **Coffee and the Italian Aperitivo**: In the early evening, the coffee bars of Perugia transform into lively aperitivo spots. While aperitivo is traditionally associated with alcoholic beverages and appetizers, some cafés offer coffee-based aperitivo options for those who prefer to keep the evening caffeine-fueled. This unique twist on the aperitivo tradition showcases the versatility of coffee in Perugia's social scene.

- **Umbria Coffee Festival**: To celebrate the region's deep appreciation for coffee, Perugia hosts the Umbria Coffee Festival, a lively event that gathers coffee enthusiasts, baristas, and roasters from near and far. The festival showcases the art of coffee making, offering workshops, tastings, and competitions that highlight the nuances of coffee culture in Perugia and beyond.

Wine Tasting in the Surrounding Vineyards of Perugia: A Journey Through Umbria's Winemaking Heritage

For wine enthusiasts and connoisseurs, the rolling hills and fertile valleys surrounding Perugia offer a haven of vineyards and wineries where you can embark on a memorable wine-tasting journey through Umbria's winemaking heritage. From robust reds to crisp whites, Umbria's diverse terroir and dedication to traditional winemaking techniques create wines that are as captivating as the landscapes they call home.

- **Wine Regions near Perugia**: The area surrounding Perugia is part of Umbria's two prominent wine regions: Torgiano and Montefalco. These regions are known for producing some of Italy's finest wines, each with its own unique characteristics and flavors.

- **Torgiano**: Torgiano, located just a short drive from Perugia, is famous for its bold and structured red wines made from the Sagrantino grape. Additionally, Torgiano is renowned for its smooth and elegant Rosso di Torgiano and white wines crafted from Grechetto and Trebbiano grapes.

- **Montefalco**: The picturesque town of Montefalco is the heart of Umbria's Sagrantino wine production. Here, you'll have the opportunity to taste powerful and age-worthy Sagrantino di Montefalco wines, which are deeply colored, rich in tannins, and exude notes of dark fruits and spices.

- **Wine Tasting Experiences**: The vineyards and wineries in and around Perugia offer a variety of wine tasting experiences that cater to different preferences. Here are some of the options you might encounter:

- **Vineyard Tours**: Join a guided tour through the vineyards, where you'll learn about the winemaking process, grape varieties, and the unique characteristics of the region's terroir. Stroll through the rows of grapevines while taking in the stunning views of the countryside.

- **Cellar Visits**: Delve into the winemaking process with a visit to the cellars, where the magic of fermentation and aging takes place. Gain insights into the art of winemaking and witness the barrels and tanks that nurture the wines to perfection.

- **Wine Tastings**: Sit down for a tasting of the winery's best wines, expertly guided by knowledgeable sommeliers or winemakers. Savor the nuances of each wine, from the aromas to the flavors, and learn about the history and stories behind the labels.

- **Food Pairings**: Many wineries offer wine tastings paired with local gastronomic delights. Sample cheeses, cured meats, and other regional delicacies that complement the wines, enhancing the overall tasting experience.

Winery Recommendations

While the options are plentiful, here are a few highly regarded wineries near Perugia worth considering for your wine tasting journey:

- **Arnaldo Caprai (Montefalco)**: A pioneer in Sagrantino winemaking, Arnaldo Caprai offers exceptional Sagrantino di Montefalco wines, as well as a range of other red and white wines. The winery provides guided tours and tastings in a beautiful setting.

- **Lungarotti (Torgiano)**: Lungarotti is a renowned winery with a commitment to sustainable viticulture. Their portfolio includes top-quality Sagrantino wines and other regional favorites. Enjoy their welcoming hospitality and diverse wine-tasting options.

- **Perticaia (Montefalco)**: Known for its modern approach to winemaking, Perticaia specializes in premium Sagrantino di Montefalco wines. Their sleek and modern winery provides a picturesque backdrop for tastings.

- **Sportoletti (Spello)**: Located near Perugia, Sportoletti is a family-owned winery that produces an array of award-winning wines, including Sagrantino and Rosso di Torgiano. Experience their warm hospitality and delightful wine pairings.

Chapter 6: Accommodations in Perugia

Luxury Hotels

Perugia and its surrounding areas boast a selection of luxurious hotels that cater to discerning travelers seeking a lavish and indulgent experience. Whether you're looking for opulent amenities, breathtaking views, or top-notch service, these luxury hotels in and around Perugia are sure to exceed your expectations:

1. **Brufani Palace Hotel (Perugia)**: Situated in the heart of Perugia's historic center, the Brufani Palace Hotel is a refined five-star hotel housed in a 16th-century palace. The hotel offers elegant rooms and suites with stunning views of the city and surrounding countryside. Guests can indulge in the

hotel's spa, fitness center, and fine dining restaurant, all while basking in the timeless charm of this historic property.

2. **Castello di Monterone (Perugia)**: Experience a stay fit for royalty at Castello di Monterone, a medieval castle turned luxury hotel. Perched atop a hill overlooking the Umbrian countryside, this enchanting property offers luxurious rooms, a swimming pool with panoramic views, and an exceptional restaurant serving gourmet cuisine.

3. **Borgo dei Conti Resort (Perugia)**: Nestled amidst vineyards and olive groves, Borgo dei Conti Resort is an exquisite five-star resort that exudes elegance and tranquility. The resort

features luxurious suites, a spa, outdoor pools, and extensive gardens. Guests can savor traditional Umbrian cuisine at the resort's restaurant, complemented by the finest local wines.

4. **Le Tre Vaselle Resort & Spa (Torgiano)**: Located in the charming town of Torgiano, Le Tre Vaselle Resort & Spa is a luxurious retreat housed in a historic 17th-century mansion. The hotel boasts beautifully appointed rooms, a spa with a Turkish bath and sauna, and a gourmet restaurant showcasing the best of Umbrian culinary delights.

5. **Nun Assisi Relais & Spa Museum (Assisi)**: Immerse yourself in history and luxury at Nun Assisi Relais & Spa

Museum. This converted 13th-century monastery offers elegantly designed rooms and suites with stunning views of Assisi. The hotel's spa, set in the ancient crypt, provides a serene space to relax and rejuvenate.

6. **Palazzo Bontadosi Hotel & Spa (Montefalco)**: Situated in the picturesque town of Montefalco, Palazzo Bontadosi Hotel & Spa is a luxurious boutique hotel housed in a historical palazzo. The hotel offers refined accommodations, a rooftop terrace with panoramic views, and a spa where guests can indulge in a range of wellness treatments.

7. **La Palazzetta del Vescovo (Spoleto)**: This enchanting country house turned

luxury hotel is located near the charming town of Spoleto. Surrounded by lush gardens and vineyards, La Palazzetta del Vescovo offers elegantly decorated rooms, an outdoor pool, and a gourmet restaurant serving delectable Umbrian cuisine.

Boutique Bed and Breakfasts

For travelers seeking a more intimate and personalized accommodation experience, Perugia and its surrounding areas offer a selection of charming boutique bed and breakfasts. These unique establishments combine the warmth of a home with the hospitality of a small inn, providing a cozy and memorable stay. Here are some delightful boutique bed and breakfasts to consider:

1. **Le Case Gialle (Perugia)**: Tucked away in the tranquil countryside, Le Case Gialle is a picturesque bed and breakfast with a rustic and welcoming ambiance. The property features elegantly furnished rooms, a beautiful garden, and a refreshing swimming pool. Guests can

enjoy a homemade breakfast with local specialties, ensuring a delightful start to each day.

2. **Il Nido dei Falchi (Assisi)**: This charming bed and breakfast in Assisi offers stunning views of the city and surrounding hills. Il Nido dei Falchi features comfortable rooms with a traditional yet stylish decor. Guests can relax in the garden or terrace, taking in the breathtaking panoramas, and enjoy a delicious breakfast with freshly baked treats.

3. **B&B Alla Residenza Domus Minervae (Perugia)**: Located in the heart of Perugia's historic center, this boutique bed and breakfast offers elegantly designed rooms with modern amenities. The

property is housed in a historic building and exudes a sense of history and charm. Guests can savor a hearty breakfast while admiring the city's ancient architecture.

4. **Residenza d'Epoca San Crispino (Assisi)**: Set within a beautifully restored medieval building, Residenza d'Epoca San Crispino offers elegant and spacious rooms with a touch of old-world charm. The bed and breakfast boasts a central location in Assisi, making it convenient for exploring the town's cultural treasures.

5. **Agriturismo Il Moro (Torgiano)**: For a tranquil countryside retreat, Agriturismo Il Moro is a wonderful choice. This charming farmhouse bed and breakfast offers comfortable rooms surrounded by

vineyards and olive groves. Guests can indulge in a wholesome breakfast featuring organic and locally sourced products.

6. **Antico Casolare B&B (Perugia)**: Nestled amidst the lush greenery of the Umbrian countryside, Antico Casolare B&B is a peaceful retreat that offers tastefully decorated rooms and a lovely garden area. The bed and breakfast serves a delightful breakfast with homemade jams and pastries.

7. **Palazzo Bontadosi Dimora Storica (Montefalco)**: This elegant boutique bed and breakfast is housed in a historic palace in Montefalco. The property features refined rooms adorned with

antique furniture and artwork. Guests can enjoy a sumptuous breakfast in the charming courtyard or elegant dining room.

Budget-Friendly Hostels and Guesthouses

For budget-conscious travelers, Perugia and its surrounding areas offer a range of affordable hostels and guesthouses that provide comfortable and wallet-friendly accommodations. These options cater to backpackers, solo travelers, and those looking to make the most of their travel budget while still enjoying a memorable stay. Here are some budget-friendly hostels and guesthouses to consider:

1. **Perugia Plaza Hotel (Perugia)**: While not a traditional hostel, the Perugia Plaza Hotel offers affordable rates for budget travelers. The hotel provides simple and comfortable rooms with essential amenities. Its central location allows easy

access to Perugia's attractions, making it a convenient base for exploration.

2. **Assisi Hostel (Assisi)**: Located in the heart of Assisi, the Assisi Hostel is a popular choice for budget travelers. This friendly hostel offers dormitory-style rooms with shared facilities and a communal kitchen. The hostel's communal areas are great for meeting fellow travelers, and it's within walking distance of Assisi's main sights.

3. **Ostello di Perugia (Perugia)**: This modern and well-equipped hostel is situated in the historic center of Perugia. It offers both dormitory-style and private rooms, providing budget-friendly options for all types of travelers. The hostel also

has a common area and kitchen, ideal for socializing and preparing meals.

4. **Locanda Paradiso Guesthouse (Assisi)**: This budget-friendly guesthouse is set in a charming medieval building in Assisi. It offers comfortable rooms with shared or private bathrooms. Guests can enjoy a continental breakfast each morning before setting out to explore the town's landmarks.

5. **B&B Al Giardino Di Alice (Perugia)**: This welcoming bed and breakfast in Perugia offers affordable rooms and a peaceful garden setting. The B&B is located within walking distance of the city center, making it convenient for exploring Perugia's attractions.

6. **Il Sentiero dei Goti (Montefalco)**: Situated in the picturesque town of Montefalco, Il Sentiero dei Goti is a budget-friendly guesthouse offering simple and cozy rooms with shared bathrooms. The guesthouse's location allows for easy access to Montefalco's charming streets and scenic views.

7. **Il Castelluccio Country Resort (Assisi)**: This countryside resort offers budget-friendly rooms in a peaceful setting. While not a traditional hostel, it offers affordable rates for those seeking a tranquil retreat in the Umbrian countryside.

Agriturismos in the Countryside

Immerse yourself in the serene beauty of Umbria's countryside by staying at one of the region's charming agriturismos. These unique accommodations offer an authentic and rustic experience, allowing guests to connect with the land, savor locally produced food, and indulge in the peaceful ambiance of rural life. Here are some agriturismos in the Umbrian countryside to consider:

1. **Agriturismo Poggio Paradiso (Perugia)**: Located just a short drive from Perugia, Agriturismo Poggio Paradiso offers a tranquil escape amidst olive groves and vineyards. This family-run agriturismo provides cozy rooms and apartments, a swimming pool with panoramic views,

and home-cooked meals featuring their own olive oil, wine, and other locally sourced ingredients.

2. **Agriturismo Il Sarale (Assisi)**: Situated in the countryside near Assisi, Agriturismo Il Sarale is a charming farmhouse surrounded by nature. Guests can stay in comfortable rooms with traditional furnishings and enjoy the beauty of the lush gardens. The agriturismo also produces its own wine and olive oil, adding to the authentic experience.

3. **Agriturismo La Coccinella (Spoleto)**: Nestled in the hills of Spoleto, Agriturismo La Coccinella offers a peaceful retreat with stunning views of the

countryside. Guests can unwind in the garden, sample the farm's organic produce, and explore the nearby villages and historical sites.

4. **Agriturismo Il Tiro (Montefalco)**: This charming agriturismo is set in the Montefalco countryside, surrounded by vineyards and olive groves. Guests can stay in comfortable rooms or apartments, take a refreshing dip in the pool, and taste the farm's wine and olive oil.

5. **Agriturismo Il Cantico della Natura (Assisi)**: Providing a truly enchanting experience, this agriturismo near Assisi is set in a restored 17th-century stone farmhouse. The property offers stylish rooms, an outdoor pool with breathtaking

views, and an organic restaurant serving traditional Umbrian cuisine.

6. **Agriturismo La Ghirlanda (Todi)**: This lovely agriturismo near Todi offers spacious rooms and apartments with rustic charm. Surrounded by olive trees and vineyards, guests can take leisurely walks in the countryside or relax by the pool.

7. **Agriturismo La Fattoria (Orvieto)**: Located in the scenic countryside near Orvieto, Agriturismo La Fattoria offers comfortable rooms, a pool with panoramic views, and a delightful garden area. Guests can enjoy farm-fresh breakfasts and explore the surrounding landscape.

Chapter 7: Shopping in Perugia

Local Artisan Crafts and Souvenirs

When visiting Perugia and its surrounding areas, you'll have the opportunity to discover an array of local artisan crafts and souvenirs that beautifully reflect the region's rich cultural heritage and artistic traditions. From ceramics and textiles to handmade chocolates and wines, here are some of the must-have artisan crafts and souvenirs to bring home as cherished mementos of your time in Umbria:

1. **Ceramics**: Umbria has a long history of pottery and ceramic production, and you'll find an abundance of beautifully crafted ceramics throughout the region. Look for hand-painted plates, bowls, and vases adorned with intricate designs and vibrant

colors. Deruta, a town near Perugia, is particularly famous for its exquisite majolica ceramics.

2. **Textiles**: Umbria is also known for its traditional textile craftsmanship. Look for woven textiles, such as colorful blankets and tapestries, as well as intricately embroidered linens and tablecloths. These textiles showcase the region's artistic flair and attention to detail.

3. **Leather Goods**: Italian leather is renowned worldwide for its quality and craftsmanship, and Umbria is no exception. Explore local shops for leather bags, belts, wallets, and accessories, all expertly crafted using traditional techniques.

4. **Perugina Chocolates**: A visit to Perugia wouldn't be complete without trying Perugina chocolates. Look for their iconic "Baci" chocolates, which are hazelnut-filled chocolate kisses wrapped in poetic messages. These sweet treats make delightful souvenirs or gifts.

5. **Olive Oil**: Umbria's fertile lands yield exceptional olive oil, and you'll find bottles of this liquid gold in various shops and markets. Look for bottles labeled with the "DOP" designation, indicating they are of protected origin and adhere to strict production standards.

6. **Wine**: As a region renowned for its vineyards and winemaking, you'll have

the chance to bring home bottles of Umbria wine. Look for Sagrantino di Montefalco, Grechetto, and other regional varietals, all of which make excellent souvenirs for wine enthusiasts.

7. **Truffle Products**: Given Umbria's fame for truffles, you'll find a variety of truffle-infused products to take home. Look for truffle oils, sauces, and even truffle-infused cheeses, all of which capture the region's unique culinary heritage.

8. **Woodcrafts**: Umbria has a tradition of woodworking, and you'll discover beautifully carved wooden objects and furniture in local artisan shops. Hand-carved wooden spoons, bowls, and

utensils are among the delightful items to consider.

9. **Traditional Crafts**: Keep an eye out for other traditional crafts such as hand-painted fans, handcrafted paper products, and artisanal soaps, each showcasing the region's artistry and creativity.

Specialty Food Stores

When in Perugia and its surrounding areas, food enthusiasts will delight in the abundance of specialty food stores that showcase the region's culinary treasures. From artisanal cheeses and cured meats to truffle-infused delicacies and fine wines, these specialty food stores offer an opportunity to take home a taste of Umbria's rich gastronomic heritage. Here are some types of specialty food stores to explore:

1. **Salumeria (Cured Meats Shop)**: Salumerie in Perugia and other towns offer a wide selection of cured meats, including prosciutto, salami, capocollo, and other regional specialties. These stores often have a variety of freshly sliced meats to choose from, making it

easy to create a delectable charcuterie platter.

2. **Formaggeria (Cheese Shop)**: Umbria boasts a variety of artisanal cheeses, and formaggerie are the perfect place to discover and sample them. Look for Pecorino, a sheep's milk cheese available in various aging stages, as well as other local cheeses like ricotta, caciotta, and aged cheeses.

3. **Enoteca (Wine Shop)**: Enotecas in Perugia and neighboring towns are dedicated to showcasing the best of Umbrian wines. Here, you can find a curated selection of reds, whites, and sparkling wines from the region's renowned vineyards.

4. **Tartufaio (Truffle Shop)**: Truffles are an integral part of Umbrian cuisine, and specialized truffle shops offer an array of truffle-infused products. Look for truffle oil, truffle sauces, truffle-infused cheese, and, of course, fresh truffles (seasonal) to take your culinary experiences to the next level.

5. **Dolceria (Sweet Shop)**: Indulge your sweet tooth at a dolcerie offering a variety of traditional Umbrian sweets. Biscotti, chocolates, almond pastries, and nougat are just a few of the treats to sample and bring home.

6. **Pasticceria (Pastry Shop)**: Pasticcerie are treasure troves of freshly baked goods.

Try a variety of delicious pastries, cakes, and cookies that showcase the finest of Umbrian baking traditions.

7. **Olio e Aceto (Oil and Vinegar Shop)**: Discover the range of Umbrian olive oils, including extra virgin and flavored oils, as well as aged balsamic vinegars. These shops often offer tastings, allowing you to find the perfect oil and vinegar pairing.

8. **Specialty Food Markets**: Keep an eye out for local specialty food markets, where vendors gather to sell a diverse selection of regional products. These markets are excellent places to interact with local producers and artisans.

While exploring specialty food stores, don't hesitate to ask the friendly staff for recommendations and tastings to fully savor the flavors of Umbria. These stores provide a wonderful opportunity to bring home authentic and high-quality Umbrian delicacies, allowing you to extend your culinary journey long after your visit to this enchanting region.

Chapter 8: Nightlife and Entertainment

Bars and Pubs

As the sun sets over the ancient streets of Perugia and its surrounding towns, a vibrant and inviting nightlife comes to life, beckoning locals and visitors alike to gather and celebrate in the city's bars and pubs. These lively establishments are the heartbeat of social interaction, offering an array of experiences that cater to various tastes and moods.

Bars in Perugia

Perugia's bars are scattered throughout its historic center, creating an enchanting ambiance as patrons spill out onto the cobblestone streets. As twilight descends, the soft glow of lanterns illuminates the facades, casting a warm and welcoming glow on the ancient buildings.

Imagine strolling through the vibrant Piazza IV Novembre, the heart of Perugia, where historic palaces frame the square and the Fontana Maggiore glows in the evening light. Along the lively streets leading from the piazza, you'll discover bustling bars with tables spilling onto the sidewalks. Here, friends laugh and clink glasses, the scent of freshly brewed coffee blending with the aroma of Italian aperitivo.

Pubs in Perugia and Beyond

For those seeking a more international ambiance, the pubs of Perugia and neighboring towns provide a cozy retreat reminiscent of the classic English pub. With wooden interiors, dim lighting, and walls adorned with vintage memorabilia, these pubs create a sense of familiarity and comfort.

Step into a quaint pub in the heart of Assisi, where a warm fire crackles in the hearth and locals and tourists alike gather around wooden tables, sipping on local beers or whiskeys from around the world. The friendly chatter of patrons creates a lively atmosphere, and the sound of live music fills the air, inviting everyone to dance and revel in the joviality.

Live Music and Entertainment

Many bars and pubs in Perugia and its surroundings offer live music, transforming the venues into stages for talented musicians and performers. From acoustic guitar melodies to lively jazz ensembles, the music spills out into the streets, captivating passersby and drawing them into the infectious rhythm.

Picture yourself stepping into a pub in the charming town of Montefalco, where the enchanting melodies of a local folk band fill the air. The captivating sound of accordions, tambourines, and traditional instruments invites you to join the locals in a joyful dance, immersing yourself in the region's rich cultural heritage.

Aperitivo culture is an integral part of the bar scene in Umbria. As the evening approaches, bars set out elaborate spreads of finger foods and appetizers, inviting patrons to indulge in the Italian ritual of aperitivo. This pre-dinner socializing is an opportunity to unwind, share stories, and savor the culinary delights of the region.

Imagine sitting in a charming bar in Spoleto, where the bartender expertly crafts an Aperol Spritz or Negroni, perfectly complementing the array of delectable nibbles on the table—bruschetta topped with fresh tomatoes, olives, cheeses, and cured meats. As the sun sets over the town's ancient walls, you raise your glass, toasting to new friendships and unforgettable memories.

Whether you're seeking a lively ambiance, a taste of international flair, or a chance to savor traditional Italian aperitivo, the bars and pubs of Perugia and its surroundings offer an enchanting and diverse nightlife that is sure to leave a lasting impression on all who embrace the experience.

Live Music and Cultural Events

Perugia and its surrounding areas in Umbria come alive with an array of live music and cultural events throughout the year, attracting both locals and visitors who seek to immerse themselves in the region's vibrant arts and entertainment scene. From music festivals to traditional celebrations, these events showcase the rich cultural heritage of the area and create an atmosphere of joyous camaraderie.

- **Umbria Jazz Festival**: One of the most renowned music festivals in Italy, the Umbria Jazz Festival, held annually in Perugia, draws music enthusiasts from all over the world. This week-long event, usually taking place in July, features an impressive lineup of jazz legends and emerging artists. The historic streets, piazzas, and theaters of Perugia become stages for soulful performances, filling the air with the captivating melodies of jazz.

- **Trasimeno Blues Festival**: Every summer, the shores of Lake Trasimeno come alive with the sounds of the Trasimeno Blues Festival. This musical celebration features a diverse range of blues and soul performances, creating a magical ambiance under the starry night sky. The festival attracts both local and international musicians, and visitors can enjoy concerts in various lakeside towns throughout the region.

- **Eurochocolate Festival**: A true delight for chocolate enthusiasts, the Eurochocolate Festival in Perugia is a mouthwatering celebration of all things chocolate. Held annually in October, this sweet extravaganza features chocolate tastings, workshops, and artistic chocolate sculptures that captivate the senses. The festival showcases Umbria's reputation as a land of fine chocolate and is an irresistible treat for anyone with a sweet tooth.

- **Umbrian Carnival Celebrations**: During the carnival season, various towns in Umbria come alive with colorful parades, music, and dance. The Umbrian carnival celebrations blend traditional folklore with lively street performances, creating a joyous and festive atmosphere. Donning masks and costumes, locals and visitors alike take to the streets to celebrate this centuries-old tradition.

- **Festa dei Ceri (Race of the Candles)**: One of the most iconic cultural events in Umbria, the Festa dei Ceri, takes place in Gubbio on May 15th every year. This ancient celebration is a thrilling spectacle where teams of strong men carry enormous wooden "ceri" (candles) through the streets, racing to reach the

Basilica of St. Ubaldo. The event is accompanied by traditional music and lively processions, capturing the spirit of the region's proud heritage.

- **Sagra Food Festivals**: Throughout the year, various towns in Umbria host sagre," or food festivals, celebrating the region's culinary specialties. These festive gatherings are an excellent opportunity to sample local dishes, cheeses, wines, and other delicacies. From truffle festivals to wine and olive oil celebrations, each sagra is a culinary journey through Umbria's diverse flavors.

- **Traditional Folk Performances**: In addition to music festivals, Umbria is known for its traditional folk performances, including "bandiere" (flag-waving), "tamburello" (drumming), and historical reenactments. These performances often take place during religious and cultural celebrations, adding an authentic touch to the region's cultural tapestry.

- **Art Exhibitions and Cultural Events**: Art lovers can also indulge in numerous art exhibitions, gallery openings, and cultural events held in Perugia and other towns throughout the year. From contemporary art to historical exhibitions, these events offer insights into Umbria's artistic legacy.

Umbria's live music and cultural events not only entertain but also provide a window into the region's soul, showcasing the passion and creativity that define its unique identity. Whether you're tapping your feet to the rhythm of jazz, savoring the sweetness of chocolate, or immersing yourself in traditional celebrations, each event invites you to connect with the heart and soul of this captivating region.

Festivals and Celebrations

Umbria is a land of vibrant festivals and celebrations that reflect the region's deep cultural roots and the joyous spirit of its people. Throughout the year, locals and visitors come together to honor ancient traditions, celebrate religious events, and revel in the artistic and culinary wonders that define Umbria's rich heritage. Here are some of the most captivating festivals and celebrations that you can experience in this enchanting region:

Infiorate (Flower Festival): Spello

In Spello, the streets are transformed into living works of art during the Infiorate, a flower festival held on the Sunday of Corpus Christi. Elaborate floral carpets, called "infiorate," are meticulously created by locals, covering the streets with intricate designs and colorful petals. The event is a beautiful tribute to the religious feast, and visitors can marvel at the ephemeral masterpieces as they stroll through the picturesque town.

Giostra della Quintana (Joust of Quintana): Foligno

The Giostra della Quintana is a medieval jousting tournament that takes place in Foligno twice a year, in June and September. Knights in historical costumes compete in a thrilling display of skill and horsemanship, aiming to hit the quintain (target) with their lances. The joust is a fascinating glimpse into Umbria's medieval past, and the town comes alive with period costumes, parades, and festivities.

Corsa dei Ceri (Race of the Saints): Gubbio

The Corsa dei Ceri, also known as the Race of the Saints, is a captivating event held in Gubbio on May 15th each year. Gigantic wooden "ceri" (candles) representing the town's three patron saints are carried through the streets by teams of runners. The race is a thrilling spectacle, and the enthusiasm of the participants and spectators creates an electric atmosphere that celebrates the city's heritage.

Umbria Jazz Festival, Perugia

One of the most famous music festivals in Italy, the Umbria Jazz Festival, held in Perugia, attracts jazz aficionados from around the world. The city's historic center becomes a stage for jazz legends and emerging artists, and the sounds of soulful melodies fill the air. The festival's joyful ambiance and world-class performances make it an unforgettable experience for music lovers.

Eurochocolate Festival, Perugia

For chocolate enthusiasts, the Eurochocolate Festival in Perugia is a dream come true. This sweet celebration showcases an array of chocolate products, from classic bars to intricate sculptures. Visitors can indulge in tastings, attend workshops, and witness chocolate-making demonstrations that highlight Umbria's reputation as a land of fine chocolate.

Perugia International Journalism Festival, Perugia

The city of Perugia hosts an internationally acclaimed Journalism Festival that gathers journalists, media experts, and the public to discuss pressing issues and challenges in the world of journalism. The festival's diverse program includes debates, workshops, and exhibitions, making it a vital platform for media professionals and an enriching experience for all attendees.

Sagra Food Festivals

Throughout the year, various towns in Umbria host sagre," or food festivals, dedicated to celebrating the region's culinary delights. From truffle festivals to wine and olive oil celebrations, each sagra offers an opportunity to savor local delicacies and experience the warm hospitality of the Umbrian people.

Religious Celebrations

Umbria's religious festivals, such as Easter processions and Christmas festivities, hold a special place in the hearts of locals. These celebrations blend faith, history, and community spirit, creating a deeply meaningful experience for both participants and observers.

From historic jousts and flower-adorned streets to world-class jazz performances and indulgent chocolate experiences, Umbria's festivals and celebrations offer an immersive and joyful journey through the region's culture, traditions, and passions. Each event provides an opportunity to connect with the heart of Umbria and its people, leaving lasting memories of the region's incomparable charm.

Chapter 9: Outdoor Activities and Nature

Walking and Hiking Trails

Umbria's breathtaking landscapes and picturesque countryside offer an abundance of walking and hiking trails that cater to both leisurely strollers and avid hikers. Whether you seek panoramic views of rolling hills, serene lakeside walks, or challenging mountain treks, the region provides a diverse array of trails to explore. Here are some of the most captivating walking and hiking routes in Umbria:

- **Assisi-MMonte Subasio**: Embark on a memorable hike from the picturesque town of Assisi to the summit of Monte

Subasio. The trail winds through lush forests, ancient hermitages, and wildflower-dotted meadows. At the top, you'll be rewarded with panoramic views of Assisi and the surrounding countryside.

- **Perugia, Sentiero degli Ulivi (Olive Tree Trail)**: Enjoy a peaceful walk along the Olive Tree Trail, starting from the historic center of Perugia. This trail leads you through ancient olive groves, offering stunning views of the city and the Tiber Valley. It's an ideal path to unwind and immerse yourself in the tranquility of nature.

- **Spoleto-PPonte delle Torri (Bridge of Towers) Hike**: The trail from Spoleto to the Ponte delle Torri is a captivating journey through nature and history. It leads you along the ancient Roman aqueduct and up to the spectacular medieval bridge that spans the deep Nera River gorge.

- **Lake Trasimeno Trail**: Explore the charming villages surrounding Lake Trasimeno on foot, following the well-marked trail that encircles the lake. The path offers delightful lakeside views, opportunities for birdwatching, and access to hidden coves and beaches.

- **Norcia**: Castelluccio di Norcia: For seasoned hikers, the trail from Norcia to Castelluccio di Norcia offers a challenging but rewarding trek through the stunning Sibillini Mountains. The route showcases wildflower-filled plains and breathtaking mountain vistas.

- **Narni-GGole del Nera (Nera River Gorge)**: The trail from Narni to the Gole del Nera takes you through ancient tunnels and bridges, offering a unique experience of walking along the Nera River gorge. The trail reveals hidden waterfalls, emerald pools, and dramatic rock formations.

- **Monte Cucco, Grotte di Monte Cucco (Monte Cucco Caves)**: The hike to the Grotte di Monte Cucco takes you to a captivating karst cave system. The trail starts in the Monte Cucco Regional Park, passing through lush meadows and beech forests, offering the chance to spot diverse wildlife.

- **Cascata delle Marmore (Marmore Waterfall) Hike**: The trail to the Marmore Waterfall takes you through lush vegetation and leads to the spectacular cascades. The waterfall's mesmerizing beauty can be admired from different viewpoints, making it a popular destination for nature lovers.

- **Gubbio-MMonte Ingino**: Hike from the charming town of Gubbio to the summit of Monte Ingino, where you'll find the Basilica of St. Ubaldo. The trail offers splendid views of Gubbio and the surrounding Umbrian hills.

- **Colfiorito Plateau**: Explore the Colfiorito Plateau, a unique landscape with high meadows and rare wetlands. The plateau is a haven for birdwatchers and offers a variety of trails that allow you to appreciate its natural beauty.

Cycling Routes

Umbria's picturesque landscapes and charming countryside make it an ideal destination for cyclists of all levels. From leisurely rides along scenic routes to challenging mountain climbs, the region offers an array of cycling routes that cater to different preferences and abilities. Here are some of the most captivating cycling routes in Umbria:

1. **Umbrian Valley Cycling Route**: This gentle and scenic cycling route follows the valley of the Tiber River, passing through picturesque towns and villages such as Todi, Deruta, and Montecastello di Vibio. The trail offers stunning views of rolling hills, vineyards, and olive groves, making it a delightful ride for cyclists of all levels.

2. **Assisi to Spoleto Cycling Path**: The cycling path connecting Assisi to Spoleto is a popular route that follows a former railway line. The path is mostly flat and takes you through tunnels and across viaducts, providing a unique cycling experience with beautiful countryside views.

3. **Lake Trasimeno Circuit**: For a refreshing ride along the lakeside, the Lake Trasimeno Circuit offers a flat route that encircles the tranquil waters of Italy's fourth-largest lake. The route takes you through charming villages, providing opportunities to stop for a lakeside picnic or visit historical landmarks.

4. **Bevagna-Montefalco Wine Route**: Cycle through the heart of Umbria's wine country on the Bevagna-Montefalco Wine Route. The trail leads you through vineyards and olive groves, passing some of the region's most renowned wineries. Along the way, you can sample local wines and savor the flavors of the region.

5. **Monte Subasio Mountain Biking**: For mountain biking enthusiasts, Monte Subasio offers a challenging and rewarding experience. The trail takes you through wooded paths and rocky terrain, providing stunning views of the surrounding countryside. The ascent is steep, but the breathtaking vistas make it worthwhile.

6. **Spoleto-NNorcia Cycling Route**: This route is perfect for cyclists who enjoy a mix of scenic beauty and historical landmarks. Starting in Spoleto and leading to the picturesque town of Norcia, the trail winds through the lush Valnerina Valley, offering breathtaking views of the Sibillini Mountains.

7. **Perugia-TTorgiano-BBettona Cycling Loop**: This scenic loop takes you through charming towns and vineyard-dotted landscapes. Starting from Perugia, the route passes through Torgiano and Bettona, offering opportunities to taste local wines and explore the region's rich history and culture.

8. **Gubbio to Assisi Cycling Trail**: This challenging cycling trail connects the medieval town of Gubbio to the spiritual city of Assisi. The route leads through undulating terrain and picturesque countryside, rewarding cyclists with captivating views and cultural discoveries.

9. **Narni-SSan Gemini-CCarsulae Cycling Route**: This cycling route takes you through the scenic Nera River Valley, passing by the medieval town of Narni, the picturesque village of San Gemini, and the archaeological site of Carsulae. The trail offers a combination of natural beauty and historical exploration.

10. **Monti Martani Cycling Circuit**: For adventurous cyclists, the Monti Martani

Circuit offers a challenging mountain ride through the Martani Mountains. The route takes you through dense forests, offering a unique opportunity to connect with nature and escape the crowds.

Lake Trasimeno Excursion

A Lake Trasimeno excursion offers a serene and idyllic escape to one of Italy's most charming lakes. Located in the heart of Umbria, Lake Trasimeno is the country's fourth-largest lake and boasts stunning natural beauty, historical landmarks, and a laid-back atmosphere. Here's a delightful itinerary for a Lake Trasimeno excursion:

Morning: Discover Passignano sul Trasimeno
Start your day by visiting the picturesque lakeside town of Passignano sul Trasimeno. Stroll along the lakefront promenade, where colorful boats gently bob on the water and small cafes invite you to sit and admire the view. Visit the medieval Rocca del Leone, a fortress

perched on a hilltop, which offers panoramic vistas of the lake and surrounding countryside.

Mid-Morning: Boat Trip to Isola Maggiore

Embark on a boat trip to Isola Maggiore, the second-largest island on Lake Trasimeno. The boat ride itself is a pleasant experience, offering beautiful views of the lake's tranquil waters. On the island, take a leisurely walk through the narrow alleys, discovering charming houses, artisan shops, and the lovely Church of San Salvatore. Enjoy a peaceful moment by the lake, perhaps reading a book or simply soaking in the serene ambiance.

Lunch: Lakeside Dining

For a delightful lunch with a view, head back to Passignano sul Trasimeno and choose one of the lakeside restaurants. Savor the region's delicious fish-based dishes, such as freshwater fish from the lake, accompanied by local wines. Enjoy the refreshing lake breeze as you relish the flavors of Umbrian cuisine.

Afternoon: Explore Castiglione del Lago

In the afternoon, make your way to Castiglione del Lago, a charming medieval town located on the western shores of the lake. Explore the town's historic center, wander through cobblestone streets, and discover medieval architecture. Don't miss the Rocca del Leone, a majestic fortress that offers splendid views of the lake and the surrounding countryside. The town also boasts artisan shops, perfect for picking up souvenirs and local crafts.

Late Afternoon: Lakeside Relaxation

As the afternoon unfolds, head to one of the public beaches or lakeside parks to relax and enjoy the tranquility of the lake. Take a leisurely walk along the shore or find a peaceful spot to watch the sunset over the water. The lake's gentle waves and golden light create a serene atmosphere, inviting you to unwind and appreciate the beauty of nature.

Evening: Sunset Aperitivo

Before leaving Lake Trasimeno, indulge in a magical sunset aperitivo. Find a lakeside bar or terrace with a view and savor a refreshing drink as the sun dips below the horizon, painting the sky with hues of orange and pink. This magical moment captures the essence of a Lake Trasimeno excursion, leaving you with lasting memories of its beauty and tranquility.

Lake Trasimeno's allure lies in its unspoiled charm, making it the perfect destination for a relaxing and rejuvenating getaway. Whether you choose to explore its islands, meander through medieval towns, or simply bask in its natural beauty, a Lake Trasimeno excursion promises an unforgettable experience in the heart of Umbria.

Chapter 10: Practical Information

Safety Tips

When traveling to any destination, including Umbria, it's essential to prioritize safety to ensure a smooth and enjoyable experience. Here are some safety tips to keep in mind during your trip to Umbria:

1. **Stay Informed**: Before and during your trip, stay informed about the current situation in the region. Check travel advisories, weather forecasts, and local news to be aware of any potential risks or changes in conditions.

2. **Travel Insurance**: Obtain comprehensive travel insurance that covers medical emergencies, trip cancellations, and other

unforeseen events. Make sure the insurance also includes coverage for any outdoor activities or excursions you plan to undertake.

3. **Secure Your Belongings**: Be vigilant with your belongings, especially in crowded places and tourist areas. Use a secure bag, keep your valuables close to you, and avoid displaying expensive items openly.

4. **Health Precautions**: Check with your doctor about any vaccinations or health precautions you should take before traveling to Umbria. Carry essential medications with you, along with a basic first aid kit.

5. **Road Safety**: If you plan to drive, familiarize yourself with local driving laws and regulations. Drive cautiously, especially on narrow, winding roads, and avoid using a phone while driving.

6. **Outdoor Activities**: If you engage in outdoor activities such as hiking or cycling, follow safety guidelines and use appropriate gear. Let someone know your plans and estimated return time, especially if exploring remote areas.

7. **Water Safety**: If you swim in lakes or pools, be cautious of the water depth and currents. Pay attention to any warning signs, and supervise children around water.

8. **Food and Water**: While the tap water in most parts of Umbria is safe to drink, it's a good idea to carry a reusable water bottle and refill it from safe sources.

9. **Respect Local Customs**: Familiarize yourself with local customs and cultural norms to avoid unintentional misunderstandings or disrespect.

10. **Language Basics**: Learn a few basic phrases in Italian, as they can be helpful in emergency situations or when seeking assistance.

11. **Use Official Transportation**: Opt for licensed taxis and official transportation services when traveling within the region.

Avoid accepting rides from unregistered or unauthorized individuals.

12. **Stay in Well-Lit Areas**: When walking at night, stick to well-lit and busy areas. If possible, travel with a companion.

Remember that safety should always be a priority during your travels.

Local Customs and Etiquette

When visiting Umbria and immersing yourself in the local culture, it's important to be aware of the region's customs and etiquette to show respect and appreciation for the local way of life. Here are some key customs and etiquette tips to keep in mind during your stay:

1. **Greetings**: When meeting someone for the first time or entering a room, it's customary to greet them with a handshake. In more casual settings among friends and family, a kiss on each cheek is common.

2. **Dress Code**: Umbrians generally dress conservatively, especially when visiting churches or religious sites. Dress modestly and avoid wearing revealing clothing in these places.

3. **Table Manners**: During meals, it's polite to keep your hands visible on the table and to wait until the host begins eating before you start. Italians often linger over their meals, so avoid rushing or asking for the bill immediately after finishing your food.

4. **Punctuality**: Italians value punctuality, so try to be on time for appointments and social gatherings.

5. **Language**: While English is widely spoken in tourist areas, making an effort to speak some basic Italian phrases is appreciated by locals. A simple "buongiorno" (good morning) or "grazie" (thank you) can go a long way in showing respect.

6. **Tipping**: Tipping is not as common in Italy as it is in some other countries. A service charge is often included in restaurant bills, but it's still customary to leave a small tip for exceptional service. In cafes and bars, it's common to leave some change when paying for a coffee or drink.

7. Respect for Religious Sites: When visiting churches or religious sites, dress modestly

and speak quietly to maintain a respectful atmosphere. Remember that these places are not only tourist attractions but also sacred spaces for worship.

8. Art of Gifting: If invited to someone's home, it's a thoughtful gesture to bring a small gift, such as a bottle of wine or a box of chocolates, for the host.

9. Respect for Property: When visiting private properties or gardens, always seek permission before entering, taking photographs, or touching anything.

10. Gesticulation: Italians are known for their expressive hand gestures during conversations. Embrace this aspect of the

culture, but try to avoid using offensive gestures.

11. Be Open to conversations. Umbrians are friendly and welcoming people. Be open to conversations with locals, as this can lead to enriching cultural exchanges and memorable experiences.

Language and Useful Phrases

Italian is the official language spoken in Umbria and throughout Italy. While many people in tourist areas speak English, making an effort to speak some basic Italian phrases can go a long way toward enhancing your interactions with locals and showing respect for the local culture. Here are some useful Italian phrases to use during your visit to Umbria:

Greetings

- Buongiorno: Good morning
- Buonasera: Good evening
- Ciao: Hello/Hi/Goodbye (informal)

Polite Expressions

- Per favore: Please
- Grazie: Thank you.

- Grazie mille: Thank you very much.
- Prego: You're welcome/Please (response to "thank you")
- Scusi or Mi scusi: Excuse me or I'm sorry (use "Scusi" for singular and "Mi scusi" for formal or polite situations).

Basic Communication

- Sì: Yes
- No: No
- Va bene: Okay/All right
- Capisco: I understand
- Non capisco: I don't understand

Asking for Help

- Mi pu aiutare, per favore?: Can you help me, please?
- Dove si trova...?: Where is...?

- Quanto costa?: How much does it cost?

Ordering Food and Drinks

- Un caffè, per favore: A coffee, please
- Un bicchiere di vino rosso/bianco, per favore: A glass of red or white wine, please
- Vorrei...: I would like...
- Il conto, per favore: The bill, please.

Directions

- Dov'è...?: Where is...?
- A sinistra: To the left
- A destra: To the right
- Dritto: Straight ahead

Numbers

- 1: Uno
- 2: Due
- 3: Tre
- 4: Quattro
- 5: Cinque
- 6: Sei
- 7: Sette
- 8: Otto
- 9: Nove
- 10: Dieci

Time

- Che ore sono?: What time is it?
- Alle (hour) e (minutes): At (hour) and (minutes)

Emergencies

- Aiuto!: Help!
- Chiamate la polizia: Call the police.
- Chiamate un'ambulanza: Call an ambulance

Remember that pronunciation is important in Italian, so listen carefully to locals and try to mimic their speech.

Emergency Contacts

In case of emergencies during your visit to Umbria, here are the essential emergency contact numbers that you should be aware of:

Police (Polizia): 112 or 113

The police emergency number in Italy is 112, which connects you to a central emergency call center. Alternatively, you can also dial 113 to reach the local police in case of any non-life-threatening emergencies or to report a crime.

Medical Emergency (Ambulance): 118

For medical emergencies, including accidents and urgent medical assistance, dial 118 to reach the emergency medical services (EMS). They will dispatch an ambulance to your location promptly.

Fire Brigade (Vigili del Fuoco): 115

If you encounter a fire or need assistance with fire-related emergencies, dial 115 to contact the fire brigade.

European Emergency Number: 112

The number 112 is a pan-European emergency number, including Italy. You can use it to reach emergency services, such as the police, ambulance, or fire brigade, from any mobile or fixed-line phone.

Carabinieri (Military Police): 112 or 112 (for general assistance), 112 for emergencies

The Carabinieri is a military police force in Italy that provides general assistance and public order.

In emergency situations, you can also dial 112 to reach them.

Roadside Assistance (Automobile Club d'Italia, ACI): 803 116

For car breakdowns or roadside assistance, you can contact the ACI (Automobile Club d'Italia) by dialing 803 116.

Remember that while many operators in Italy may understand and speak English, it's beneficial to have some basic knowledge of Italian to communicate effectively during emergency situations. Always stay calm and provide clear information about the location and type of emergency when making an emergency call. Additionally, keep your travel insurance information and emergency contacts readily accessible in case you need to seek assistance during your trip to Umbria.

Chapter 11: Day Trips from Perugia

Assisi

Assisi is a charming medieval town located in the region of Umbria in central Italy. It is renowned for its historical and religious significance as the birthplace of Saint Francis of Assisi, one of the most beloved and revered saints in the Catholic Church. The town's rich history, stunning architecture, and spiritual atmosphere attract visitors from all around the world. Here are some of the highlights and must-visit places in Assisi:

- **Basilica di San Francesco (Basilica of Saint Francis)**: The Basilica of Saint Francis is the most significant religious site in Assisi and a UNESCO World Heritage Site. It consists of two main churches, the Upper Basilica and the Lower Basilica, both adorned with stunning frescoes depicting the life of Saint Francis and other religious themes. The basilica is a pilgrimage destination for Christians and a place of profound spirituality.

- **Rocca Maggiore (Assisi Castle)**: Perched on the hill overlooking the town, Rocca Maggiore is a medieval fortress with a fascinating history. It offers breathtaking views of Assisi and the surrounding countryside. Exploring the castle grounds and climbing its towers is a memorable experience.

- **Basilica di Santa Chiara (Basilica of Saint Clare)**: Dedicated to Saint Clare, a follower of Saint Francis, this basilica holds her relics and offers a serene and peaceful atmosphere. The basilica's simple beauty and lovely rose garden attract visitors seeking moments of reflection and prayer.

- **Piazza del Comune (Town Square)**: The heart of Assisi is Piazza del Comune, a lively square surrounded by historic buildings, cafes, and shops. It is a great place to relax, enjoy Italian gelato, and soak in the ambiance of the town.

- **Temple of Minerva (Tempio di Minerva)**: This ancient Roman temple, dating back to the 1st century BC, is remarkably well preserved and is now used as a church called Santa Maria Sopra Minerva. It stands as a testament to Assisi's rich history, blending ancient Roman architecture with Christian traditions.

- **Basilica di Santa Maria degli Angeli (Basilica of Saint Mary of the Angels)**: Located at the foot of the hill of Assisi, this grand basilica houses the tiny Porziuncola Chapel, where Saint Francis founded the Franciscan Order. It is one of the most important pilgrimage sites in the Franciscan tradition.

- **Eremo delle Carceri (Carceri Hermitage)**: Nestled in the wooded slopes of Mount Subasio, Eremo delle

Carceri is a peaceful and secluded hermitage where Saint Francis and his followers sought solitude and contemplation. The hermitage offers hiking trails and the opportunity to connect with nature.

- **Assisi Underground (Assisi Sotterranea)**: Explore the hidden subterranean passages and tunnels beneath Assisi to learn about its ancient history and see the remains of Roman structures and water systems.

- **Art and Craft Shops**: Assisi is known for its artisan shops, where you can find beautiful religious art, handmade ceramics, textiles, and other local crafts.

Take the time to browse and find unique souvenirs.

Assisi's spiritual and historical significance, combined with its stunning architecture and picturesque setting, make it a truly enchanting destination. Whether you come for religious reasons or simply to immerse yourself in the town's timeless beauty, Assisi will captivate your heart and leave you with lasting memories.

Gubbio

Gubbio is a captivating medieval town located in the northeastern part of Umbria, Italy. Nestled in the Apennine Mountains, Gubbio is renowned for its well-preserved historical architecture, picturesque streets, and rich cultural heritage. It's a town that exudes charm and offers visitors a step back in time. Here are some of the highlights and must-visit places in Gubbio:

- **Palazzo dei Consoli**: Standing tall on the main square, Piazza Grande, Palazzo dei Consoli is an impressive Gothic palace that now serves as the Town Museum (Museo Civico). It houses various artifacts and exhibits showcasing the town's history, including ancient Roman artifacts, medieval art, and more. The rooftop terrace provides breathtaking views of Gubbio and the surrounding landscape.

- **Basilica of Saint Ubaldo (Basilica di Sant'Ubaldo)**: Perched atop Mount Ingino, the Basilica of Saint Ubaldo is a significant religious site and a symbol of Gubbio. Inside the basilica, you can see the remains of Saint Ubaldo, the town's patron saint. The basilica is also home to the Ceri, tall wooden structures used during the Corsa dei Ceri festival.

- **Cathedral of Gubbio (Duomo di Gubbio)**: The Cathedral of Gubbio, dedicated to Saints Mariano and Giacomo, boasts a stunning façade and an impressive collection of religious art and relics. Its Gothic architecture and beautiful interiors make it a worthwhile stop on your visit to Gubbio.

- **Palazzo Ducale**: Palazzo Ducale is an imposing Renaissance palace that once served as the residence of the Dukes of Urbino. Today, it houses the town's offices, but visitors can still admire its grand architecture from the outside.

- **Roman Theater and Amphitheater**: Discover Gubbio's ancient Roman past by visiting the Roman Theater and Amphitheater. These well-preserved archaeological sites are a testament to the town's ancient origins.

- **Piazza Grande**: The main square, Piazza Grande, is the heart of Gubbio's social and cultural life. It is surrounded by beautiful medieval buildings, cafes, and shops, making it a delightful place to stroll and soak in the town's atmosphere.

- **Cable Car to Mount Ingino**: Take a cable car ride up to Mount Ingino to visit the Basilica of Saint Ubaldo and enjoy panoramic views of Gubbio and the surrounding hills.

- **Eugubine Tablets (Tabulae Eugubinae)**: The Eugubine Tablets are ancient bronze inscriptions dating back to the 3rd and 1st centuries BC. They provide valuable insights into the ancient Umbrian language and culture.

- **Corsa dei Ceri (Race of the Saints)**: If you visit Gubbio on May 15th, you can witness the Corsa dei Ceri festival, a thrilling and historic event where teams of locals carry the Ceri through the streets in a lively procession.

Spoleto

Spoleto is a picturesque town located in the southern part of Umbria, Italy. With its rich history, stunning architecture, and scenic surroundings, Spoleto offers visitors a perfect blend of art, culture, and natural beauty. From ancient Roman ruins to medieval landmarks and cultural events, Spoleto has much to offer. Here are some of the highlights and must-visit places in Spoleto:

- **Rocca Albornoziana (Albornoz Fortress)**: The imposing Rocca Albornoziana is a medieval fortress that dominates the town's skyline. Built in the 14th century, it offers panoramic views of Spoleto and the surrounding countryside. Inside, you'll find the National Museum of the Duchy of Spoleto, housing a collection of archaeological artifacts and art.

- **Duomo di Spoleto (Spoleto Cathedral)**: The Spoleto Cathedral is a magnificent example of Romanesque architecture. Its intricate façade and impressive bell tower make it one of the most significant religious sites in the town. Inside, you can admire stunning frescoes and religious artworks.

- **Ponte delle Torri (Bridge of Towers)**: The Ponte delle Torri is an ancient aqueduct and bridge that spans the deep Nera River gorge. Dating back to Roman times, the bridge offers spectacular views and is an iconic symbol of Spoleto.

- **Teatro Romano (Roman Theater)**: The Roman Theater is an ancient archaeological site dating back to the 1st century BC. It was once a venue for performances and events. Today, visitors can explore the well-preserved ruins and imagine the theater's grandeur in ancient times.

- **Basilica of San Salvatore**: This early Christian church is a UNESCO World Heritage Site and an exquisite example of Lombard architecture. The interior features beautiful frescoes and a serene atmosphere.

- **San Pietro Church (Chiesa di San Pietro)**: Located just outside the town's walls, San Pietro Church is another example of Romanesque architecture. Its unique façade and beautiful interior make it a hidden gem worth visiting.

- **Spoleto Festival dei Due Mondi (Festival of the Two Worlds)**: One of Italy's most prestigious cultural events, the Festival of the Two Worlds, takes place in Spoleto every summer. It showcases a diverse array of music, dance, theater, and art performances, attracting artists and spectators from around the world.

- **Palazzo Comunale (Town Hall)**: The Palazzo Comunale is an elegant medieval building located on Piazza del Mercato. It houses the town's administrative offices and features a lovely courtyard.

- **Santa Maria della Manna d'Oro**: This church is famous for its Golden Chapel, adorned with a stunning 5th-century mosaic depicting scenes from the life of Christ.

- **Stroll through the Historic Center**: Wander through Spoleto's narrow cobblestone streets, lined with charming cafes, shops, and historic buildings. The town's enchanting atmosphere invites leisurely strolls and exploration.

Spoleto's wealth of historical and cultural treasures, combined with its breathtaking landscapes, creates a captivating destination that leaves visitors with unforgettable memories. Whether admiring ancient ruins, attending cultural events, or simply enjoying the town's serene ambiance, Spoleto promises a delightful experience in the heart of Umbria.

Orvieto

Orvieto is a captivating hilltop town located in the southwestern part of Umbria, Italy. Perched high atop a tuff cliff, Orvieto offers stunning panoramic views of the surrounding countryside and is renowned for its rich history, beautiful architecture, and cultural heritage. The town's medieval charm and unique Etruscan and Roman influences make it a fascinating destination to explore. Here are some of the highlights and must-visit places in Orvieto:

- **Orvieto Cathedral (Duomo di Orvieto)**: The Orvieto Cathedral is a masterpiece of Italian Gothic architecture and one of the most remarkable cathedrals in Italy. Its striking façade features intricate sculptures and colorful mosaics. Inside, visitors can admire stunning frescoes, beautiful stained glass windows, and the Chapel of San Brizio with its impressive Last Judgment frescoes by Luca Signorelli.

- **Pozzo di San Patrizio (St. Patrick's Well)**: The Pozzo di San Patrizio is an engineering marvel, designed by Antonio da Sangallo the Younger in the 16th century. This well has an impressive double helix structure that allows for easy access to water from different levels without crossing paths. Visitors can descend into the well and marvel at its construction.

- **Orvieto Underground (Orvieto Sotterranea)**: Explore the fascinating underground tunnels, caves, and chambers that lie beneath Orvieto's historic center. These hidden spaces offer insights into the town's ancient Etruscan and medieval pasts.

- **Palazzo del Popolo**: The Palazzo del Popolo is a medieval palace on Piazza del Popolo. It is now the town hall and houses the civic museum (Museo Civico). Visitors can explore the museum's art and archaeological collections, as well as enjoy panoramic views from the palace's tower.

- **Orvieto's Etruscan Heritage**: Learn about Orvieto's Etruscan origins at the National Archaeological Museum of Umbria, which displays a collection of artifacts from the Etruscan era. Additionally, visit the nearby Etruscan necropolis (Necropoli Etrusca) to see ancient tombs and burial sites.

- **Church of San Giovenale**: This small Romanesque church dates back to the 9th century and is one of the oldest in Orvieto. Its simple beauty and historical significance make it worth a visit.

- **Orvieto's Wine**: Don't miss the opportunity to taste the region's renowned Orvieto Classico wine. Numerous wine cellars and enoteche (wine shops) in town offer wine tastings and the chance to purchase local vintages.

- **Orvieto's Cuisine**: Indulge in the local gastronomy, which includes traditional Umbrian dishes such as truffles, wild boar, and handmade pasta. Be sure to try the region's signature dish, "Umbrichelli al Tartufo" (pasta with truffles).

- **The Scenic Walks**: Explore the town's medieval streets, archways, and charming alleyways. Stroll along the town's walls for stunning views of the surrounding countryside.

Orvieto's unique blend of historical heritage, art, and scenic landscapes makes it a must-visit destination in Umbria.

Chapter 12: Conclusion

Final Tips and Recommendations for Your Trip to Umbria

- **Travel Insurance**: Before traveling to Umbria, ensure you have comprehensive travel insurance that covers medical emergencies, trip cancellations, and other unforeseen events. Check if your insurance includes coverage for outdoor activities you plan to undertake.

- **Pack Accordingly**: Umbria's climate can vary throughout the year, so pack clothes suitable for the season. Comfortable walking shoes are essential, especially when exploring historic towns with cobblestone streets.

- **Cash and Cards**: While major credit cards are widely accepted, it's a good idea to carry some cash, especially for smaller establishments or when visiting rural areas.

- **Public Transport**: If you plan to use public transportation, familiarize yourself with the schedules and routes. Trains and buses are convenient for traveling between towns and cities.

- **Respect Religious Sites**: When visiting churches and religious sites, dress modestly and speak quietly to maintain a respectful atmosphere.

- **Try Local Cuisine**: Umbria is known for its delicious food and wine. Don't miss the chance to try local specialties like truffles, wild boar, and Umbrian wines.

- **Language**: While English is spoken in tourist areas, learning some basic Italian phrases will enhance your interactions with locals and show appreciation for the culture.

- **Beware of Pickpockets**: Like in any tourist destination, be cautious of your belongings in crowded places and tourist hotspots.

- **Tipping**: Tipping is not as common in Italy as in some other countries. It's appreciated but not mandatory. If service is exceptional, leaving a small tip is a nice gesture.

- **Stay Hydrated**: Carry a reusable water bottle and stay hydrated, especially during hot weather.

- **Stay Safe at Night**: Stick to well-lit and busy areas when exploring at night. Travel with a companion whenever possible.

A Fond Farewell to Perugia

As the time comes to bid farewell to the enchanting city of Perugia, a flood of emotions fills the heart. The memories of strolling through its historic streets, savoring delectable Italian cuisine, and immersing oneself in its rich culture linger like cherished treasures. The sight of the majestic Palazzo dei Priori and the buzzing atmosphere of Piazza IV Novembre become etched in the mind, forever intertwined with the joyous laughter of newfound friends.

In Perugia, time seems to dance at its own pace, allowing each moment to be savored like a fine wine. The sunsets that bathe the city in golden hues, casting a warm glow upon its medieval walls, become moments of serenity and reflection. The vibrant soul of Perugia, infused with art, history, and a palpable sense of community, finds its way into the heart, leaving an indelible mark.

As the final footsteps echo through the stone alleys, gratitude fills the soul for the experiences shared with locals and fellow travelers alike. The heartfelt "arrivederci" from the friendly barista at the local café, the warm smiles exchanged with shopkeepers, and the camaraderie found in exploring hidden gems all contribute to a tapestry of cherished memories.

Yet, a fond farewell to Perugia is not just a parting; it is an invitation to return someday, to reunite with the city's soulful charm. The promise to revisit the Etruscan arch, wander through the art-filled halls of the Galleria Nazionale dell'Umbria, and savor the delight of a gelato in Piazza Italia lingers in the heart like a sweet melody.

As the journey continues beyond Perugia's ancient walls, the essence of the city remains intertwined with one's own journey of growth and discovery. The spirit of Perugia becomes a cherished companion, inspiring a newfound appreciation for the beauty that lies in embracing different cultures and celebrating the human connections that bridge distances.

So, as the sun sets over the rolling hills of Umbria, casting its farewell embrace upon Perugia, the heart brims with gratitude for the memories made and the experiences lived. Fond farewells are merely stepping stones to new beginnings, and Perugia, with its timeless allure, becomes a chapter of life forever cherished, promising to welcome all who return with open arms and an invitation to create new memories in the embrace of its magical embrace once more.

Printed in Great Britain
by Amazon